Scenery for Your
Model Railroad

Mike Danneman

Photos by the author unless otherwise noted

KALMBACH
BOOKS

Printed in the United States of America

03 04 05 06 07 08   10 9 8 7 6 5 4 3 2

Visit our website at
http://kalmbachbooks.com
Secure online ordering available

Publisher's Cataloging-in-Publication
(Provided by Quality Books, Inc.)

Danneman, Mike, 1963–
    Scenery for your model railroad, from tabletop
to backdrop / Mike Danneman — 1st ed.
    p. cm.
    ISBN 0-89024-323-9

    1. Railroads—Models. 2. Miniature craft.
I. Title.

TF197.D36 2000   625.1'9
                    QBI00-901538

Book design: Sabine Beaupré
Cover design: Kristi Ludwig

Contents

Acknowledgments

First, I want to thank my parents, Herb and Mary, for giving me my interest in railroads and skills in art. I feel grateful to be able to combine both in my life's endeavors.

Thanks to all of the modeler/photographers who have helped me with this book: Eric Brooman, Ron Hatch, Homer Henry, Joe Lesser, Allen McClelland, Bill and Mary Miller, Marty McGuirk, Bill and Wayne Reid, George Sebastian-Coleman. Without the help of these people, this book would have been incomplete.

I also thank Dave Frary, who helped make the water-soluble method of scenery construction popular. Thanks to all the modelers in the past who messed with plaster and screen, those who zip- and zap-textured, and those who just plain tried anything that might work for scenery building. We have all learned from their trials and tribulations. They have made scenery and layout construction the art it is today.

This book is one way to explore scenery and backdrop construction. There are other methods that can be used to create that miniature world of railroading, and there will be other methods in the future. What's important is to have fun today and to enjoy building scenery and painting your backdrop.

Introduction

You've spent countless hours designing and constructing the layout you've always wanted to build. First you assembled the supportive benchwork, then you laid and wired the track. You even detailed some of your rolling stock in preparation for the first running train on your layout. The first several times the train runs around the layout are perhaps the most satisfying moments in model railroading. But as time goes on, you begin to recognize that your layout differs from what you had originally envisioned.

You've recognized that scenery is perhaps the most important unifying element in model railroading. Detailed rolling stock, beautiful structures, and perfectly laid track are all bound together with scenery to create a miniature world of railroading. And the more effective and realistic the scenery is, the more believable the rest of the elements will be.

Backdrops are scenery components that help create a realistic overall scene. Even if the foreground scenery is spectacular, your attention will gravitate to the cinderblock walls, the copper pipes, or anything else just behind the hills and trees. A nicely finished backdrop together with the scenery will provide the perfect stage to showcase the trains you have built and detailed so carefully. It will become a complete railroad in miniature. The backdrop also comes in handy if you plan to photograph your model railroad.

In this book, I'll show you some of the best methods available for creating realistic scenery that emphasizes backdrops. As with any building projects, there will always be several ways to do things. Don't feel that you have to be an artist to create great-looking scenery or backdrops. Some of the same materials and techniques used for scenery are also used in successful backdrops.

Many other books on model railroad scenery have already been published. I highly recommend Dave Frary's *How to Build Realistic Model Railroad Scenery*. This book covers Dave's water-soluble methods of creating scenery, which are the basis of many of today's scenery techniques. Also handy is *Scenery Tips and Techniques* from *Model Railroader* magazine. This is a collection of favorite scenery articles from the pages of *Model Railroader*, and it contains some unique methods of scenery making by different authors.

Feel free to experiment with the scenery. Use a technique that is comfortable to you. It's hard to make a fatal mistake when you're working on scenery. After all, scenery in the real world is often imperfect. So get those materials out and start modeling the scenery you've always wanted for your layout!

Chapter • One

The function of a backdrop

When it comes to creating a realistic model railroad, nothing goes as far as good scenery and a backdrop. Just as any good theatrical production has appropriately attired actors working with realistic props in a credible setting, a great model railroad should have detailed models operating through and around lifelike structures, scenery, and backdrops to be believable.

Picture this view without any scenery or backdrop. There would be nothing but a few trains and some track. The mind can conjure up a make-believe scene for the train to run through, but this gets old after a while. Add two important ingredients like scenery and a backdrop to the recipe, and you get a complete railroad scene in miniature.

Top: A BNSF coal train winds through scenic Wendover Canyon in Wyoming. A prototype railroad scene can be inspiring not just for the train itself, but for the country it runs through.

Above: Even if you don't have room for the entire engine facility on your layout, don't despair. Look at what Joe Lesser did on his hi-rail JL/ATSF layout. The diesel house is painted on the backdrop behind the roundhouse! Good blending of the scenery and the backdrop complete the illusion.

Left: The prototype hills beyond this station scene of Pagosa Junction are too far away to model with scenery. Some hills and a few lazy clouds were painted on the backdrop to complete the scene.

Even if the layout is no wider than a shelf, a big scene can be constructed. This view on the Kalmbach Publishing Co. employee layout is not very deep at all. A painted backdrop of rolling farmland increased the depth of the scene.

Consider for a moment what constitutes an ideal railroad setting. Most likely you'll visualize more than just trains and structures—perhaps you envision some nice scenery and background. Maybe lazy cumulus clouds float overhead. Or distant rolling mountains beckon another trip over the pass. Maybe evergreens cover the hillside, or there is a craggy rock cut for the train to travel through. The scenery and especially the backdrop play a big part in our overall perception of the railroad and its association with the real thing. Let's look at a few ways a backdrop can work to enhance the scenery and your entire layout.

Backdrops to extend the scenery on your layout

Having a backdrop on the layout expands its apparent size. A nicely painted backdrop makes the layout seem bigger and is sometimes the only way to get in all of the scenic elements you want. Building flats can expand the size of the city. Mountains can expand the size of a canyon the track winds through. You might be surprised just how well a simple rolling hillside painted on a backdrop works to create the illusion of a larger landscape for your trains to run through.

Backdrops to hide unfinished walls

Backdrops placed behind the layout along the walls can serve a dual function. First, they enhance the realism of your railroad. Perhaps even more important, they disguise any ugly distractions such as cinder-block basement walls or other rough construction that you might find in an attic, basement, or garage. In these instances, it's much more economical and attractive to add a backdrop than it is to finish off walls using sheet rock or paneling that will eventually be hidden behind a backdrop anyway.

Backdrops on narrow, shelf-type layouts

Even if you have a very narrow, shelf-type layout, the backdrop can be effective in creating a scene. Say a portion of the layout is only 12 inches wide. When you add a backdrop of rolling hills, sky, clouds, and trees, the depth of the scene grows from 12 inches to infinity. In fact, most of the scenery can actually be replicated on the backdrop, leaving the shelf for trains.

Helpful Hint #1 When designing a layout that includes backdrops, try to visualize the layout from the viewer's perspective. One way to help you imagine how a backdrop can help a scene is to construct a small, simple scale model of the layout. Although it is somewhat time-consuming, making this model can shed light on future ideas that might or might not work. Many people are turning to the computer for this step of the layout design process. Several good layout design programs are now available.

When you look at prototype photographs, look at the background of the photo. Note how the background subjects in it relate to the position of the backdrop on your layout. Could certain structures be modeled as "flats" on the backdrop? (A flat is one wall of a building.)

Top and above: A double-sided backdrop constructed from a hollow-core door divides the small layout in half. Two different scenes were constructed, one on each side, effectively making the layout twice as large. Some scenery painted on the backdrops made the layout seem even bigger.

The backdrop for this scene on the HO Milwaukee, Racine & Troy layout was installed and painted blue as part of the benchwork construction. But the backdrop was painted after installing the track, bridge, and scenery. Painting rolling hills and clouds around the finished models was a little tough. Take care to prevent any damage to the surrounding models when painting a backdrop on a finished layout.

Backdrops as scenic dividers

Backdrops certainly work well along the outside walls of the layout room, but they also are great as scenic dividers in other areas of your layout. A peninsula on a layout can be divided in half to create two separate scenes. Using a backdrop in this fashion allows your track to run through two different scenes. The distance your trains travel will seem greater, thus effectively increasing the realism of the layout.

Placing a backdrop in the middle of a turnaround loop is also a great way to conceal some unrealistic, but necessary, segments of track. When you look at a peninsula without a backdrop, a loop of track looks just like what it is, a loop of track. Often the prototype does not have a loop of track in the area you are modeling. But by installing a double-sided backdrop down the center of the peninsula, you effectively divide the loop into two regions and eliminate the problem of a non-prototypical loop.

Planning for the backdrop

The backdrop is something to consider when you are in the earliest phases of layout construction. It's a good idea to treat backdrop construction much like finishing off a room or basement in preparation for the layout. Just after you have installed lighting in the layout room is an ideal time to know at least where you'll want to include backdrops. With the lights functioning, you'll be able to mitigate any shadow effects and lighting hotspots on the backdrop. Preplanning layout lighting in concert with the backdrop will save a lot of headaches later. By preplanning, you can build the backdrop at the same time as the benchwork. Just be sure to leave enough access in the benchwork so you can comfortably reach the backdrop for painting.

Right: A loaded coal train with a gold and silver caboose passes a Rio Grande freight with five units on the point. Notice an afternoon rainstorm brewing on the backdrop. Sure is nicer to look at than a plain old wall!

Below right: This overall view of part of my new Rio Grande layout shows how a central double-sided backdrop can be used to separate scenes. The fluorescent lighting is arranged so that the layout areas are as evenly lit as possible. Additional track lighting highlights certain areas of the layout and supplements other areas that need a little more light than the fluorescent provides.

What if your layout is already built? You can still add a backdrop. It'll take some elbow grease and a bit of patience, but in the end it will be worth it. Once you decide where the backdrop will benefit the layout most, you'll need to remove enough scenery to allow you to fasten the new backdrop in place. Once the backdrop is place, you can easily blend it in with the scenery.

Painting a backdrop on a finished layout can be quite a challenge too. Covering the layout with a lightweight dropcloth will help preserve finished scenery, but painting in hard-to-reach areas is not especially easy to do. In such cases you might want to prepaint your scenery onto the backdrop before installing it on the layout, making sure to consider how your finished scenery will blend with your backdrop.

By far, the most sensible way to accommodate a backdrop on your layout is to consider how it will function as an integral part of the complete model railroad in your initial layout plan. Just like everything else about the layout—from the track to the rolling stock and from the scenery to the control system—the backdrop is a significant piece of the model railroad puzzle. Layout visitors won't overlook it, and neither should you.

Chapter • Two

Considering the scene

If you're preparing to build scenery, you probably already know what prototype (real) railroad you want to model. It may be a favorite because of the motive power, the paint scheme, or even the scenery it runs through. Knowing what railroad you want to model will help determine what type of scenery you will build. Even if you're building a freelanced railroad (one not based on a prototype railroad), you'll still have to decide what type of scenery your layout will portray. The most believable freelanced railroads are ones that appear real in more ways than just a realistic paint scheme.

The inspiration for this N scale scene came from the proto-type Rio Grande. South of Malta, Colorado, on the Tennessee Pass line there is a small trout pond called Crystal Lake. From the lake, the beautiful Rocky Mountains rise up to the west. Two of Colorado's largest peaks, Mount Elbert and Mount Massive, dominate the range.

Above: When I built the N scale Rio Grande, I added a scene inspired by this view. In the prototype scene, SP KCOAF passes Crystal Lake on the morning of August 2, 1996.

Eric Brooman

Left: Utah Belt OAGAZ is eastbound with a stack train at Cortez Point. It almost sounds as though we are talking about a real railroad rather than Eric Brooman's HO scale layout. Above: A Southern Pacific westbound coal empty passes Finger Rock on the Craig Branch in Colorado. Such a peculiar rock formation on a model railroad would be too unbelievable and probably shouldn't be modeled.

Modelers have developed many great freelanced railroads by selecting a region of the United States, adding a railroad, and surrounding it with plausible industries and scenery. By carefully including the correct scenery for the region you are modeling, you will make your freelanced railroad far more credible. Take a close look at the region, and you'll find many scenic details, including industries, that will help portray a realistic scene. It would be awfully tough to model a sawmill in desert scenery or plunk down a grain elevator in Rocky Mountain scenery! Allen McClelland's Virginian & Ohio and Eric Brooman's Utah Belt are a couple of outstanding examples of a well-conceived freelanced layout.

Seek the common ground

Even though it is very tempting to model some of nature's breathtaking phenomena, don't do it. While you can attempt to model the beautiful red rock natural arches of Utah or the Grand Canyon of Arizona, no matter how well you model spectacular scenery like this, it will look unbelievable in comparison

Right and below right: Another source of inspiration for my Rio Grande layout came from this view on the Moffat line at Crescent, Colorado. I pretty much free-lanced the scenery to fit the area on the layout. But I did use the photo as a source of inspiration.

to the real thing. Try to model more typical scenery. In most instances, the more common the scenery is in real life, the more believable the miniature scenery will be. This isn't to say you should never try to replicate some specific unique scenery found in the areas you are modeling, but you should think about how believable the scenery will be when scaled down.

Gather inspiration and information

Whether you are freelancing a railroad or modeling your favorite prototype down to the tie, you'll want to use as many references as you can find. If you can go out into the field to see the real railroad and the scenery it runs through first-hand, it will surely help you portray the prototype accurately. Even if the railroad you are modeling has been merged into history, or even worse, abandoned, a visit to the area will still provide many scenic ideas and hints.

Photos from books, magazines, videos, and Internet sites about the railroad you are modeling will also supply a wealth of modeling references. You'd be surprised how many modeling ideas you can gather from the pages of *Trains* magazine or picture books like Kalmbach's *Golden Years of Railroading* series. What follows is a selection of prototype railroad photos to inspire your scenery and backdrop.

Top: Four Soo Line Geeps head across America's Dairyland at Van Dyne, Wisconsin. The flatlands of the Midwest cry out for some backdrop painting to give the modeled scenes an open feel.

Above left: Conrail pushers enter famous Horse Shoe Curve in Pennsylvania. The rolling mountains of the eastern United States are known for their incredible colors in autumn. Don't forget to include some greener trees among the brilliant colors.

Above right: The rolling, tree-covered hills of Missouri are the backdrop for this Santa Fe intermodal train heading west at the tiny town of Ethel. If you're modeling some parts of the eastern U.S., a thick cover of foliage will make the hills look realistic.

Right: A Canadian National run-through train cruises along the Mississippi River in the BNSF mainline to Chicago. Notice how dark the color of the water is from above.

Top: An eastbound Burlington Northern coal train, with both BN and Soo Line power, east of Medora, North Dakota. Note the interesting colors of the rocks in this area, which is close to the Badlands.

Above left: The incredible Bookcliff mountains shadow much of the old Rio Grande mainline around Thompson, Utah. Mountains like this painted on the backdrop take more time, but are well worth the effort.

Above right: Autumn can be a great time to model, as this photo of BNSF number 4 east of Havre, Montana, can attest. But be cautious of using too much colorful foliage. Even in the peak fall color weeks, much of the foliage is shades of brown and green.

Left: The double-track line over Crawford Hill in Nebraska is a conduit for coal trains. You can re-create a hazy sky using lighter acrylic shades as you paint closer to the horizon.

Chapter Three

Constructing a backdrop

There are several good methods you can use to build your backdrop. No one is correct, and you may even develop your own alternative method. No matter which you choose, I do recommend that you construct your backdrop first. Somewhat like starting with the foundation of a house before building the walls, the best time to construct the backdrop is at the beginning of layout construction. Just be sure to leave enough space through the benchwork for you to access the backdrop and work freely on it. Let's look at some points you'll want to consider before you begin construction.

Even on a small layout, such as the Alkali Central, the backdrop becomes an important part of layout design and construction. This backdrop is a piece of hollow-core door positioned on the center of the layout, effectively dividing the 4 x 8-foot layout into two different scenes.

The JL/ATSF Railway layout of Joe and Jo Lesser is built as a piece of furniture in the living room, and the backdrop supports that idea. Notice how the backdrop doesn't have to be overly tall to be effective.

Heisler number 8 drifts downgrade across the Elk Mountain Timber steel trestle on Bill and Mary Miller's On3 layout. They used linoleum to construct their backdrop, with great success.

Backdrop height

Should you go all the way to the ceiling with the backdrop, or not? If the backdrop is entirely around the outer walls of the basement or layout room only, why not go all the way to the ceiling? But if you are using double-sided backdrops on a island or peninsula-shaped layout, leaving 12 inches or more between the top of the backdrop and the ceiling will help keep air circulating throughout the room. The backdrop really doesn't have to be all that tall to be effective, but you'll want to keep it as close to eye level as possible.

Backdrop tools

The tools you will need for constructing the backdrop are the basic construction tools you use on the rest of your layout. Wallboard used for backdrops can be cut with a circular saw. I have used an orbital jigsaw for this too, but straight cut lines are a little more difficult to do. You can use the same jigsaw for cutting plywood roadbed and fascia profiles, so the investment is well worth it. You will also need a basic circular saw (or miter saw) to cut any dimensional lumber used for supporting the backdrop.

I find that having two variable-speed reversible drills is handy too. One drill is for drilling pilot holes, and the other is equipped with a bit for driving drywall screws home. A third drill actually would have been nice for use with a counter-sink bit to get the screwheads flush with the backdrop surface. I ended up getting pretty good at switching bits.

Also necessary for the finishing process of the backdrop is mud (joint compound), joint tape, and a 12-inch wallboard knife for applying the mud. Patching the screwheads with mud is a must, but the backdrop vertical joints are optional. I recommend patching them too for maximum finished look and realism.

Backdrop materials

One of the more useful materials used for backdrops is ⅛-inch wallboard (also sometimes known as hardboard). This material is generally available in 4 x 8-foot and 2 x 4-foot sheets. Wallboard works so nicely because it can be curved around corners so that your backdrop will have that museum diorama quality with no visible corners. I have bent a curved backdrop to a radius of about 12 inches without breaking by applying a bit of plain tap water to the front and back surfaces of the wallboard with a sponge. The water helps warp the wallboard material to the curve you want.

Support the backdrop with furring strips placed every foot or so. You can attach these strips directly to the outer walls of the layout room or to the back of the layout. You can also build a double-sided backdrop on small layouts or larger layout peninsulas by sandwiching the furring strip supports between two sheets of wallboard.

Another material you might want to try is styrene. This material is available in different thicknesses and comes in rolls. A visit to a building supply store will help you decide which thickness to buy. Test the "curvability" of the material. Try to buy the thickest sheet that will curve around the corner radii that you will use but still be manageable enough to "hang" from the supports behind your layout. For most situations, I'd recommend using sheets .060 inch thick.

The basic support of furring strips will work fine. But instead of using nails to install your styrene, try using an adhesive like Liquid Nails. Make sure the adhesive does not attack the styrene so much that it shows on the finished side. Test the adhesive with a scrap piece of material before you start.

With styrene, I definitely recommend sanding the surface before painting. Sanding gives

Construct a backdrop

Constructing a backdrop need not be difficult. The first decision is how high to make the backdrop. There is no set height, but you'll want to leave a gap of a few inches between the top of the backdrop and the ceiling to allow some air to circulate to hidden staging and access areas.

After cutting the backdrop material (in this case, wallboard) to the proper height, mount it directly to the studs in the wall behind, or to a framework of 2 x 4s placed vertically every 16 inches if you are installing the backdrop against a cinderblock basement wall. You can use smaller dimensional lumber, depending on the height of your backdrop.

I attached my wallboard backdrop with 2-inch drywall screws. The first step is locating the support stud and marking the location with a small pencil mark. Then drill a pilot hole with a 7⁄64 drill bit. Use a countersink bit to allow the drywall screw head to lie flush with the surface of the wallboard. Then drive home the drywall screws. One quick reminder: leave a tiny space between each wallboard section for expansion and contraction. A penny on edge put between wallboard pieces works well.

The next step is to patch the seams between the wallboard section and cover the screw heads. The method here is the same as the one wall finishers use in home construction. Mud (Joint compound), joint tape, and a wallboard knife are the supplies you'll need.

After finishing the mud-and-tape process, apply a primer coat to give the backdrop a nice even surface for the blue sky color. I used some pure-white flat latex paint left over from another household project, but any latex wall primer will do. Two coats covered the difference between the dark brown of the wallboard and the stark white of the patched areas.

Then paint the backdrop with the sky blue of your choice. I decided to add a slight gradation of the blue from dark to light, top to bottom. This step is not necessary, but it is effective in representing the gradation seen in the sky toward the horizon. Use two tones of blue paint, with one being slightly darker. This is definitely a two-person effort. One person applies the dark and light blue on the backdrop. The other follows with a four-inch paint brush and quickly blends the two together. Any areas that don't get blended very well can be covered with clouds.

In this area of Denver Union Station on the new Rio Grande layout under construction, the backdrop is installed directly to the walls and post. The area behind this is hidden staging and access.

Countersink pilot holes for these screws, then drive them flush to the surface of the wallboard. Apply the first layer of mud over the joints and the drywall screws.

Tape the joints and apply more mud over them. Three coats of mud are generally necessary for the best coverage of the joints and screws.

After coating the backdrop with two coats of primer to seal the mud and give the surface an even color, paint it sky blue. The backdrop is now ready for further painting.

Let there be light

Eric Brooman

Eric Brooman

The way a layout is lighted has a big effect on how the scenery and trains will appear. Compare these two photos of Eric Brooman's Utah Belt. Both scenes are identical except for the lighting. The angle of the light on the rocks and scenery varies greatly. What type of lighting you like is a personal preference, so experiment and find the lighting that works for you.

Lighting can affect how well the scenery blends into the backdrop. These two photos show how different lighting angles affect the trees close to the backdrop. In the first view, these trees cast unrealistic shadows on the backdrop. In the second photo, the angle of the lighting is changed to get rid of the tree shadows, helping to blend the scenery into the backdrop.

the slick styrene surface some tooth for the successful adhesion of paint. Even with sanding, the styrene won't have the same durability that wallboard will. This is something to consider if your backdrop will get any rough handling during its lifetime.

Linoleum for the backdrop surface has its advantages. A support of wood is necessary, as with any other method. But where linoleum shines (no pun intended) is that it is available in very long rolls, eliminating the vertical joints that occur with other surface materials.

Use the least expensive linoleum possible. When shopping for it, check the back side or smooth side—that is what will be the surface of the backdrop. You don't want some nice mosaic texture all over your sky, do you? Enjoy the funny looks from the salesman as you check out the bottom surfaces of the linoleum.

Attach the linoleum to the support with Liquid Nails. This will eliminate any need to patch those nail holes. Roll the glued joints with a wallpapering roller for smoothness. Latex paint will stick directly to the linoleum surface. If you have any doubts about its adhesion, a light sanding of the surface before painting should help.

Use a wallpapering technique for the seams. Overlap the two sections that will butt together. Slice through both pieces with a sharp utility knife edged with a metal straightedge to keep the seam even. Remove the excess material. Now apply glue up to these seams and roll the joint with a wallpapering roller to get a very clean cut.

You could use other materials for the backdrop. Thin sheet metal is one possibility, but I don't recommend it. Metal is harder to cut and it takes a lot of trouble to attach it to vertical surfaces. Often latex paint doesn't adhere to the surface of metal

Enlightening scenarios

Be sure to consider the lighting for the layout right after you construct the backdrop. Once the backdrop is up, areas that need more or less light will be readily apparent. Installing the lighting is much easier now than after most of the layout is constructed, as you can see in the following examples from my layout.

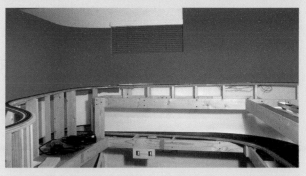

Because I wanted to keep the basement window accessible, I didn't want to cover it with the backdrop. I decided to paint the blinds covering the window with the sky blue I used on the backdrop. It really didn't look too bad. The window also was a good place to raise the height of the backdrop for the higher portion of the layout to the right.

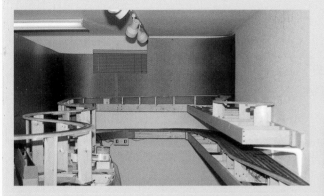

The two fluorescent light fixtures in the upper left of the photo straddle the top of a double-sided backdrop. This didn't work because it caused light "hotspots" on the backdrop. I replaced the lights with fixtures that parallel the peninsula on both sides of the backdrop (see photo on page 11).

Notice how the track lighting installed here helps highlight a future part of the layout. The nice thing about track lighting is that you can change and move it as the layout progresses.

without a lot of surface prepping. Don't be afraid to experiment with materials, but just make sure that they fit your criteria for the finished look that you are after for your backdrop.

Lighting

Layout lighting is very important to the presentation of the scenery and backdrop. I prefer lighting that gives a nice even look to the overall scene. Incandescent bulbs will work, but they can become expensive to operate and generate plenty of heat. Banks of fluorescent tube lighting are more economical, but the light can have many tones. Getting fluorescent bulbs that most closely match the 5000K lighting of the outdoors is

the best way to go. These bulbs are, however, more expensive.

Another popular technique is using regular fluorescent lighting overall with occasional spot lighting with incandescents. This gives the layout fairly even lighting and appears nicely color balanced. Always be aware of where your roadbed and scenery will be to get the best lighting.

On small layouts a system of track lighting works nicely. The only drawback of this system on larger layouts is the expense of the necessary number of track lights. Your main goal is even layout lighting. That way the scenery and backdrop will look most realistic. Just as in viewing and photographing real trains, the best light is low angled light. Try to

make sure you are not just lighting the tops of your trains, but are also casting some light on the sides. You want light that best shows off your trains and scenery.

Always seek professional electrical help if you have any lighting problems or questions. You might try asking someone at a lighting store or home improvement center what they might suggest. I've found that they often find the lighting challenge of a model railroad very interesting, and can really help solve any of your questions. It is also a good idea to have the same type of lighting at your workbench. This way, any models you build, paint, and weather at the workbench will have the same color tone as the layout.

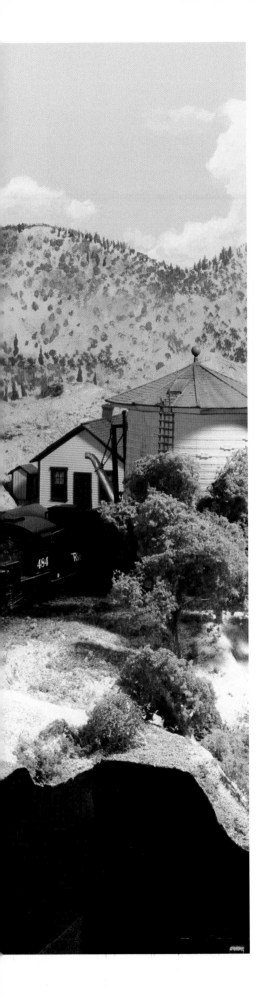

Chapter Four

Painting the backdrop

Now that the backdrop is in place, it's time to apply some color. Now you're going to paint a backdrop. I know, I know, you say you're not an artist. While that may be true, you're not going to try anything all that challenging. Since the backdrop is in the background, it doesn't have to be a detailed work of art. What you will try to capture is the feeling of scenery in the distance.

Denver & Rio Grande Western narrow gauge K-36 484 leads a freight past the Pagosa Junction depot on the HOn3 layout of Herb and Mike Danneman. The backdrop here was painted first, before anything else on the layout.

Backdrop colors

Titanium White

Mars Black

Burnt Sienna

Raw Sienna

Burnt Umber

Raw Umber

Payne's Gray

Ultramarine Blue

Brilliant Blue

Hooker's Green

Chromium Oxide Green

Yellow Oxide

Cadmium Yellow

Cadmium Red

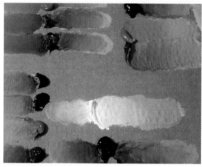

Above: Mix acrylic paints with both the scenery base color and the sky blue color on a scrap piece of cardboard. This will give you a good idea of what colors you can make with these combinations. Save this piece of cardboard, and refer to it if you have any questions about color mixtures.

Distant mountains and clouds, faraway rolling hills and meadows, or hazy shapes of trees don't require a lot of time and effort to paint. In this chapter, I will show you step-by-step how to capture some common scenes on your backdrop. The techniques use common artist's acrylic paints mixed with household latex paints. Both can be used and mixed together with great results.

Above: This prototype view of a Santa Fe intermodal at Essex, California, shows how little detail is visible in the background mountains. Miles and miles of diffusion make them easier for the backdrop painter to replicate.

Don't be afraid to give it a try. If the backdrop doesn't turn out the way you want, just paint it blue and start again. Let's gather a few supplies.

Acrylic paints

Any art store sells acrylic paints, and many hobby shops do too. The brand name is not important. What's important is having a selection of colors that will give you the right tones on the backdrop.

At left is my list of the best colors to buy for backdrop painting. Note that some colors will be used in large quantities, and others in very small amounts. When blended with white and black, the four browns of sienna and umber should give you any tone of brown you need. You'll have to mix many colors get the desired shade. The key is to have these colors and use a mixture of them to create any shade or color you need. Remember, you will use these colors as tints in conjunction with the base color and sky color. To paint a large backdrop area entirely with acrylic paints would require a lot of little acrylic tubes, so you'll want to save your money by using latex paint for your base and sky color.

The key to successful colors on a backdrop is mixing tones to blend with the foreground scenery. The best way to get the right color is to apply all of your colors to a palette (I use old pieces of cardboard) and mix the colors you need to get the desired tone. The darker the color, the closer it will appear on the backdrop. The lighter the tone, the farther it will appear. Keeping this in mind will help in choosing the right colors.

There really isn't an exact science to blending colors. The best thing you can do is just dive in and mix an assortment of colors together and see the results. The best way to gain knowledge about the acrylic paint is to experiment. Your eye will tell you what looks right and what doesn't.

Brushes

The best brushes to use on your backdrop also come from an art store or hobby shop. Some of the larger round and filbert-style work best. Brushes are numbered; the smallest numbers are the smallest brushes. Brushes like 0, 00, and 000 are awfully small, and you won't need them here. The best brushes for the backdrop are sizes 4 to 8 and up. I even use regular house-painting brushes for large areas. Acquire a variety of sizes and shapes. They are expensive, but with proper care and cleaning, they will last quite a while. More expensive brands such as Winsor and Newton, and Grumbacher do last longer.

Choose a variety of sizes and shapes of brushes. The synthetic white acrylic brushes last the longest and work best with the paints.

Other supplies

Sponges can be used for applying paint. While I prefer to use brushes, sponges are especially good for clouds because they create a random pattern. Several old buckets (like plastic sherbet and ice cream containers) filled with warm water are all you need for thinning and washup. When the water becomes tinted, it's time to get some fresh stuff. Keep plenty of rags handy for spills, drying brushes, and so on. I use plain paper towels for this purpose too.

Preparing the backdrop and scenery base

After you've primed the backdrop surface with a few coats of white or light-colored latex paint, the next step is to paint your entire backdrop with a pleasant blue color to represent the sky. What color is that, you ask? It depends on the region of the country you are modeling and what effect you are after. The color of the sky of an Appalachian summer day is perceptibly different from the sky of an autumn day in the Rockies of Montana. This is where photos of a particular area and prototype are a great help. Look through many photos and select a color that looks right to you. I recommend using a flat latex interior paint. It's most likely that the color will have to be custom-mixed, so get enough to cover the entire backdrop area plus some extra for painting scenery. I use extra blue latex paint mixed with acrylic scenery colors to paint the backdrop, which I'll describe later.

You can roll or brush the blue sky color over the backdrop. Rolling the paint will yield a

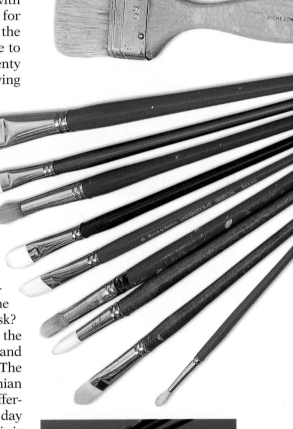

Different brushes work best for certain applications. In the photo above, bottom row, left to right; two flat brushes, a round brush with flat tip, a round brush with a pointed tip, two filbert brushes, and a small round brush. The three brushes at the top are worn out, to say the least. But those old brushes are great for certain applications.

Mountains, on the other hand, usually have much clearer weather and bluer skies. Pick a blue color to match the type of sky commonly seen in the country of the prototype you are modeling.

ing. Or it could be a gray to match the rocks. Pick a color based on samples collected within the area you're modeling or a color commonly seen in photos. You'll also want to use it for the backdrop as a base color.

Beginning the backdrop scenery

I usually start painting scenery by sketching some of the distant land forms on the backdrop with colored chalks. These chalks are available at any art store. By doing this, you can get an idea of where you want the background forms before actually committing to them with paint. You can remove the chalks with a sponge and water and then redraw them.

You can use your own slides of the prototype to assist in painting the backdrop. Maneuver your projector with the slide in place

better surface and a nicer surface for painting the backdrop. You'll probably need two coats—just like painting the house. When you're finished, you'll notice how the backdrop already makes the layout room look better. Just think what it will look like with

some distant scenery added to it!

When modeling actual scenery on your layout, consider covering the scenery forms (foam, hardshell, and so on) with a coat of scenery-base-colored latex paint. The color could be a tan to match the dirt in the area you're model-

Sky blue?

The sky color you pick for your layout is a subjective one. The shade (how deep the blue is) depends on the area of the country you are modeling. Also the room light will have an affect on the tint. I went to several different paint store nearby, and took swatches of all of the colors I thought were close to "sky blue." I took them home and leaned them up on the backdrop with all of the layout lights on. The different shades of blue were staggering. Just take your time and pick one that looks right to you.

Picking a sky blue color can be an exercise in patience. The color I picked is somewhere in those paint samples.

Above: Place the acrylic paints in a ring on a scrap piece of cardboard. Arrange the colors loosely by type. Letting the dabs of different color paints touch is okay. Use the center area for mixing the colors together. Here I am mixing a good green color for background trees.

Right: I bought the chalks in this box at an art supply store. The sticks were sold separately, so I picked up a box of colors in natural earthy colors. These chalks also double as my weathering chalks.

so that the projected subject appears appropriately sized on the backdrop. Then lightly sketch the scenery directly onto the backdrop by tracing features in the photo. Make sure that trees and other features are not out of scale with your models in the foreground. Dim room lighting works best for this process, since you need to see both the backdrop and the slide image.

Painting with acrylics

After sketching the land forms with chalk, it's time to start painting. Before you actually start covering the backdrop of your layout with paint, you might want to experiment with the acrylics to see how they handle. Acrylics are thinned with water like latex paints. (This is why they work so well in conjunction with ordinary latex paints for painting backdrops.) If you experiment with the two together to see what kinds of effects are possible, there will be fewer surprises when you start the real thing.

Arrange all of your acrylics in a ring on the palette. Arrange them by color groups, keeping similar hues closer together. Put only small amounts of acrylics on the palette, because they dry quickly. Using a paintbrush, try mixing several different colors with your sky blue color and your base color to see what tones result. Don't be afraid to experiment with the colors.

When you're ready to work directly on the backdrop, paint the most distant scenery first, moving forward to the closest scenery. The most distant scenery will always be lightest in color, and the closest scenery will be darkest. However, the closest scenery on the backdrop should not be darker than the actual modeled scenery. As you work with these paints, you'll find that the color dries slightly darker than when it is applied. This is the nature of acrylic paint, so keep it in mind when you're painting backdrops. You'll see exactly what to do as you work through the following step-by-step backdrop painting projects.

Why acrylic paints?

Acrylic paints are perfect for painting backdrops. They are fast-drying, opaque, and permanent. They mix with water, have minimal smell, and can be painted over if you make a mistake. Many factors will help you decide what colors and shades to use and mix. What area of the country do you model? Should the sky be a pale blue, like the color you'd see on a humid July day on the East Coast, or is the sky a deep azure, like the color you'd see on a western mountain pass? The same can be said for the colors of the scenery painted on the backdrop. And most of all, it depends on how the layout is lighted. Fluorescent lighting will change the look of a color compared to incandescent lighting.

Acrylic paint tips

Even though the colors and tones of the backdrop are purely a personal preference, some techniques and tips will get you started in the right direction. The first thing to keep in mind is that acrylics dry fast. Squeeze an inch or so out of a tube and experiment with it. Smooth it out with a brush as you would if you were painting a wall. Note how fast it dries. The thinner you coat a surface with acrylics, the faster it will dry. The fast drying time is beneficial, however, when you are painting in layers.

Painting in layers is easy with acrylics. If you use a technique like "paint by numbers," each color butts up to the next. Painting in layers allows you to overlap each color. Because acrylics are opaque and dry so fast, it is possible to paint in layers. You can add to the backdrop as you go. You can paint trees over distant hills with no problem. Foreground hills can overlap or even obliterate the background ones.

You could use oils to paint your backdrop, but they take much longer to dry than acrylics—sometimes even months!

Blending paints

Dab some of your sky blue color and some of the scenery base color onto a scrap piece of cardboard. Mix the two together to see what happens to the tone. I normally use the brush I will paint with to mix the colors together (even though it may eventually wear down the brush). Now squeeze a dab of all of the acrylic paints you will use in painting the backdrop around the sky and base colors. Intermix them and see what colors are formed. Notice how well acrylics blend with other acrylic colors and with the latex colors. This is the best way to see what colors you will need for the backdrop. Notice how varying the amount of acrylics with the latex changes the darkness and tone.

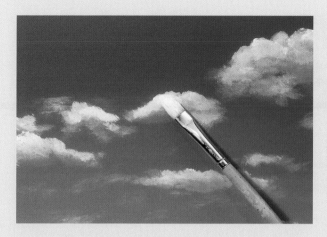

Using acrylic paints for backdrops is a natural. The ability of acrylic paints to be applied in layers makes it easier to correct mistakes. Notice how the white is opaque enough to cover the deep blue.

Different brushes and strokes will yield different results. Some examples, from top to bottom: (1) house-painting stroke, (2) stippling stroke, (3) drybrushing stroke, (4)scrubbing stroke.

I wish there were a scientific way to measure the colors and the amounts of paints you need, but there just isn't. Don't throw this piece of cardboard out. Save it for when you want to know what color to use for a specific purpose. It can become your color wheel when you want to know how to achieve a certain color or tint. The color might just be on that scrap, giving you a much better chance of getting a close match.

Other pointers about acrylics

Acrylic paints have other properties too. One thing to keep in mind is color tint. Acrylics are similar to latex paint in this respect—they always dry slightly darker than when wet. If you ever wonder which color tint to use, always err on the light side.

When mixing acrylics, never mix more than you will use in a short amount of time, since they dry so fast. There is no way to use dried acrylic paint. Any left after a painting project will just be discarded. Start by squeezing out a small volume of paint that's about the size of a Hershey's kiss.

What if the drying time is too fast? You can buy a tube of Retarding Medium at the art supply store or hobby store. You can slow drying time by mixing the medium with acrylics up to 25 percent by volume. You may find that Retarding Medium makes the acrylics too transparent and shiny when dry. This is not desirable on your backdrop; you could fix it by overspraying the area with a light coat of Dullcote lacquer. Experiment first before you try Retarding Medium on your backdrop.

Different strokes

Different brush strokes also have an affect on the finished look of applied acrylics. Four different brush strokes are generally used.

House-painting stroke: Use a large brush (flat or round) to spread the paint over a large area. It is much like painting a house, only you use horizontal strokes. Avoid using vertical strokes on the backdrop unless you're depicting a tree or some other vertical subject.

Stippling stroke: Trees are often painted with this stroke. For example, take a medium-size brush and load it up with paint. Apply the paint with a dabbing motion at a 90 degree angle to the surface. Experiment with different pressures to apply different amounts of paint. Sometimes the worse shape the brush is, the better it is for stippling.

Drybrushing stroke: Rub the same brush you used for stippling on some scrap paper or cardboard to remove most of the paint from brush. Now lightly stroke the surface you want to paint. Notice how a tiny amount of paint shows, mostly on the high part of the surface. This is drybrushing. Varying the amount of paint of the brush will change the effect.

Scrubbing stroke: This is similar to both stippling and drybrushing, only you use a scrubbing action to apply the paint. Some of the color from the previous layer can show through. Scrubbing is a great way to get color applied without a definite edge. Like stippling, this technique can be very hard on brushes. Sooner or later you will have designated brushes for these jobs.

A Rocky Mountain backdrop

Some of the most spectacular North American railroad scenery is in the heart of the Rocky Mountains. This type of scenery is popular with modelers, for obvious reasons. This series of step-by-step instructions shows how easy it is to add similar mountains to your own backdrop.

The photos show the On3 Denver, South Park and Pacific layout under construction by George Sebastian-Coleman. Only the backdrop and sub-roadbed are complete. At this point there is plenty of access to the backdrop for painting, and since the position of the track is now known, it is easy enough to decide where the backdrop scenery should be.

The modeled region is the Woodstock area with Sherrod

This O scale narrow gauge scene of the famous Denver, South Park and Pacific is being built by George Sebastian-Coleman. The backdrop was painted before a single spike was driven, allowing much better access to the backdrop.

Curve and the Palisades section of South Park, Colorado. George took some fine photos of the area, and they were invaluable in painting the backdrop. A few of these prints, some showing the abandoned grade and surrounding area, could be matched with photographs taken 100 years ago. Obviously, the colors of the scenery haven't changed, so we relied on George's photos for the colors. Note that all of the areas that will be covered with real scenery were painted in George's base color.

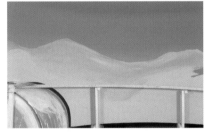

1 The first step is to sketch where the mountains will be on the backdrop with chalk. You can simply sponge away any mistakes or revisions. You can also try to airbrush white paint lightly in the sky near the horizon of the scenery. An aerosol can of white will work too, but be sure to keep the spray at a fine mist that feathers into the blue sky. Adding this effect to the horizon makes for a more prototypical clear sky. This also helps make the clouds look more realistic.

2 Rough in the distant mountain scenery with a mix of base color, sky color, and small quantities of brown, gray, and white acrylic paints from your palette. It is better to err on the light side at this point, since the colors can always be darkened later. Use photos of the real thing as a reference.

3 Using base color tinted with browns and black, start texturing the surfaces of the mountains. These darker areas represent distant shadows and boulder fields and give the mountain its shape. Picking a scenery base color is similar to picking a sky color. Base the color you pick on the preponderant color of earth in the area you are modeling.

4 In the previous photo you'll notice a dark area in the saddle between the two peaks. I didn't think this looked quite like the prototype photos, so I added some lighter colors and quickly covered up the mistake. That is the beauty of acrylic paints; dark colors cover light colors, and light cover dark.

5 Paint more layers of different shades (or "textures") with subtle mixes of grays, browns, yellows, and reds to create more shape on the mountains. Detail is not necessary, but these subtle lights and darks will help define the shape of the scenery. Remember here that the goal is not to cover each texture, but to subtly blend each with the next.

6 The huge stands of pines are best painted using a stippling stroke to apply a mixture of base paint tinted with black, brown, and Hooker's green. Make sure that the color used for the trees is lighter and slightly bluer than the model trees that will eventually be blended in the foreground. Remember, lighter shades look more distant.

7 Use different amounts of green and brown to vary the colors of the trees. Small amounts of black can be used too, picking out subtle shadows between trees.

This closeup photo of the main mountain above Sherrod Loop on George's layout shows that the painting doesn't have to be super-detailed to be effective. When the backdrop is seen from a normal viewing distance, the missing detail will not be visible. Some snow may be added later, but since this area is closer to the layout's edge, it can be done at any time. (Paint snow with straight titanium white, with a little blue mixed in here and there to represent shadows.)

Helpful Hint #1   In general, household latex paints dry to a lighter color, and artist's acrylic paints dry to a darker color. Since background painting sometimes mixes latex paint with acrylic paints, you will frequently get different shades of color when the paint is dry. When painting backdrops, let the paint dry in one area before moving on too far to the next. Make sure you have the tones that you want. Darkening or lightening the colors of the backdrop scenery isn't that difficult once you know how to handle the individual paints.

Southeastern mountain scenery

Wayne Reid

Greencastle, Pennsylvania, on the N scale Reid brothers' layout is a perfect example of eastern and southeastern mountain scenery. Notice the very effective rolling hill disappearing into the backdrop scenery.

The rolling mountain of the South and Southeast are not all that difficult to paint. Keeping the terrain rolling and the colors soft are the keys to success. Because the Mountains of the eastern United States are much older, they are much tamer in feature. And because the weather in this part of the country is much more humid, they are covered with trees. This makes the backdrop painting easier than the actual scenery. To do the scenery right, the mountains have to be covered with thousands of trees. Painting trees on the backdrop is much easier.

The humidity of this part of the country also changes the way the scenery appears. The backdrop, including the sky, should be more subtle and lighter in color. By paying close attention to these factors, you can create a more realistic southeastern mountain backdrop like the one that I added to Homer Henry's HO scale layout under construction. The scenery is a generic representation of the southeastern mountains. Homer follows no specific prototype but wants the right overall feel for the area. Most of the layout will have scenery, but a few areas looked right for a bit of backdrop painting.

1 Using sheets of pink insulation, rough in all areas you'll want for actual layout scenery. These areas represent how far up the backdrop the scenery will be. Doing this helps you visualize the actual scenery and helps eliminate areas of the backdrop that don't need painting.

2 Paint the most distant mountains first. Use the sky color with a small amount of blue and green. Test the color. It should be just slightly darker than the sky if you want it to look like a very distant mountain.

3 Layer the mountains forward. By adding darker mixes of the blue and green to the sky color, you will make the mountains appear darker on the backdrop. The darker they are, the closer they appear. Continue to do this until you cover the area of the backdrop that needs mountains. Bring the mountains completely down to the edge of the pink foam. Some closer trees stippled along this edge will help blend the backdrop into the scenery.

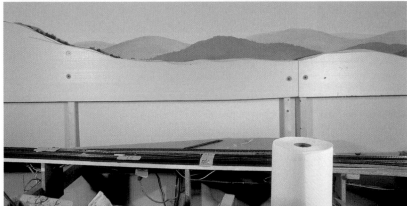

4 Now, add some clouds to the scene. Since the sky is a perfect faded blue, like those hazy, hot summer skies so prevalent in the Southeast, the clouds won't stand out too much. But the addition looks great. Use white blended with the sky color to paint the tops of the clouds, and blend a small amount of Payne's gray to the underside.

5 A look at a scene of the layout under construction after the backdrop is in place shows that the backdrop already gives the scene some depth. Doing the backdrop first like this really helps the modeler visualize the completed scene. Once the scenery is started in front of the painted backdrop, the emphasis on the backdrop is reduced, and your eyes properly focus on the main subject at hand, the railroad. This is why it is so important to not put a lot of detail in the backdrop.

Painting clouds

Everyone could use some clouds on the backdrop. Here are some prototype photos to help you paint clouds.

A UP freight hustles eastbound at Maxwell, Nebraska, under some picture-perfect clouds. Use Payne's gray for the darker tones in clouds like these.

Santa Fe 5378 east heads into Abo Canyon, New Mexico. Scrub and drybrush white acrylics to simulate these wispier clouds. Some final touch-up with an airbrush will bring it all together.

C&NW Dash 8s head west out of Maxwell, Nebraska, under a mostly cloudy sky. This many clouds are not usually painted on backdrops, but it would be fun to see someone try.

Clouds are something every layout can use, even if you don't want anything else painted on your backdrop. And because clouds come in so many random shapes and different sizes, they are not all that hard to do. I use either titanium white acrylic paint or ordinary white latex house paint. If you use latex house paint, be careful what tone the white really is. Many white house paints are not truly white but are tinted. Choose the whitest and flattest white latex. The best test of the whiteness of your paint is to compare it to a small amount of titanium white. Some tint to the color isn't bad, but the truer the white, the "cleaner" the clouds will look.

Pour some of the sky blue color into a disposable cup. Do the same with the white color. Also put a small amount of Payne's gray on a palette.

Payne's gray works well for the lower shadowed side of the clouds.

Using a large brush, dab white where you want the cloud. Use the sky blue color to feather the edges on portions of the cloud. This helps alleviate the chunky look of the clouds when they're painted with the straight white. Use a rolling, scrubbing motion with the brush to create the clouds. You can even use drybrushing for the thin, wispy clouds.

Blend small amounts of Payne's gray mixed with white and sky blue for the underside of the clouds. A small amount of Payne's gray goes a long way, so use it sparingly.

Paint the larger clouds toward the top of the backdrop, working smaller and smaller clouds toward the horizon line. The clouds also get closer

Some classic thunderheads building in the distance at Edgemont, South Dakota. Hard edges on the tops of the clouds are accented with plenty of gray underneath.

A scattering of clouds in the Mojave desert at Fenner, California. Notice the different sizes of the clouds and how they get smaller toward the horizon.

Sometimes the clouds overlap near the horizon, as over this Santa Fe eastbound at Goffs, California.

A pair of BNSF SD75Ms gathers speed heading out of the mountains at Blackfoot, Montana. Sometimes the clouds are not are well defined, making them harder to paint, as in this view.

together as they get closer to the horizon. Keep the pattern of the clouds random; don't put clouds everywhere. Grouping them seems to help. For further photo references, take a few pictures yourself the next time you have one of those beautiful skies filled with pretty, white puffy clouds near your home. These photos really do come in handy when you're painting clouds.

You can paint clouds on a backdrop with sponges. The random shape of a sponge works well to duplicate the random shape of clouds. Tape pieces of sponge to the end of a stick to get to those hard-to-reach places on a finished layout. You have less control over how you apply the paint, but you can get excellent results by painting clouds with a sponge. Instead of scrubbing and drybrushing, which is what you do with a stan-

dard brush, you use a dabbing motion with the sponge, letting the rough edges of the sponge define the shape of the cloud. Rotate the sponge for a variety of shapes for the clouds.

Another technique for painting clouds is using a couple of spray cans of white and gray paint. Make sure this paint is flat and can be sprayed to a fine mist. An airbrush works well for this too. Cut stencils or frisket to the shape of clouds. Vary these greatly for the most realism. Hold these masks ¼ to ½ inch from the backdrop and lightly spray the clouds in place. Experiment with the amount of paint to apply to get the result you are looking for. Apply a light dusting of gray to the bottom with the same technique. The nice thing about these clouds is that you can always go back and feather them with a brush.

New England autumn backdrop

Marty McGuirk

Spectacular New England foliage abounds on Marty McGuirk's N scale Central Vermont.

All the beautiful colors of a crisp fall day make it tempting to model an autumn scene on a layout. But you've got to be careful when modeling all those bright colors. You can model the season successfully by carefully controlling how much color you use. If you look closely at the fall foliage, you'll probably notice how far apart the richly colored trees are spaced. Use this same spacing on the autumn foliage on your layout and backdrop, and I think you will be pleased with the results.

Marty McGuirk's N scale version of some beautiful fall scenes along the Central Vermont cries out for some backdrop painting to tie everything together. Vermont lends itself perfectly to modeling the autumn season.

1 Start this project by adding modeled trees to help you visualize the final scene and to help match and balance the colors on the backdrop. You can remove the trees to make painting the backdrop easier and replace them at any time to check on your progress. It is helpful to rough in the basic ground cover too.

2 Paint the distant rolling mountains at the proper height on the backdrop. The color is mostly the sky blue color, mixed with a small amount of ultramarine blue, green, and brown. Make sure the color is light enough that it is only slightly darker than the sky blue color. How dark depends on how far away you want the mountain to look. Even thought he time is fall, no fall color will be visible at the distance of the mountain, so don't fret about all the colors

3 It's time to add the closer mountains. Mix scenery base color with some sky blue and small amounts of brown and green acrylics. Remember that the background will always be lighter than the foreground. This is a base coat; you'll add other colors on top of this color to give some texture to the mountains.

 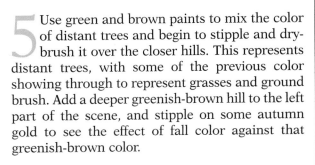

4 Now start adding some subtle effects of fall foliage with yellow oxide, burnt sienna, and any other colors that represent the fall color in the area you're modeling. Remember to keep these subdued by mixing them with the scenery base color.

5 Use green and brown paints to mix the color of distant trees and begin to stipple and dry-brush it over the closer hills. This represents distant trees, with some of the previous color showing through to represent grasses and ground brush. Add a deeper greenish-brown hill to the left part of the scene, and stipple on some autumn gold to see the effect of fall color against that greenish-brown color.

6 The last step is to add the touches of fall color that help blend the backdrop with the modeled trees. Use red, yellows, and greens (or whatever other colors you have planned for the modeled foliage) and stipple them onto the backdrop to represent closer trees. For a really bright tree, the color might be straight out of the tube. But don't overdo the bright colors.

Establishing the proper horizon height

The proper height for the horizon is also subjective. Knowing the angle at which you view your trains will help. If you look down at your models (most layouts have this viewpoint), then the horizon should be slightly lower than your eye level. If you are a taller individual, you might want to lower it more for an average person.

On a mountain scene, for example, the closer the mountains are to the viewer, the taller they will be on the backdrop. If they are very far away, they will be lower to the bottom of the backdrop. The painted areas of the backdrop should never be taller than the modeled scenery or buildings, unless they represent taller scenery painted on the backdrop because the modeled scene is very narrow, such as on a shelf layout. This may sound sort of confusing, but since many factors are at work here, some experimenting will help.

Cut out some simple cardboard forms to represent the scenery you will paint on the backdrop. You can even paint them to represent a close approximation of the scenery. Vary the height of these forms and look at them in comparison to the models in the foreground. This is a great way to fine-tune the perfect horizon line for your backdrop scenery.

The rolling hills of Wisconsin are quite easy to duplicate. Green mixed with the sky color works well for distant trees. Stipple closer trees onto the backdrop using a green close to the color of the future three-dimensional trees.

Joe Lesser

The toy train layout of Joe Lesser features museum-quality backdrops that enhance the realistic appearance of the scenery.

Other types of backdrop scenery

Don't be afraid to try paint other types of backdrop scenery. The flat country of the Midwest cries out for the backdrop to give the scene more space. Painting the rolling hills of the Kettle Moraine area of Wisconsin is not all that different from painting the mountains of the East. Study prototype photos of the area you are modeling and adapt the type of scenery you see for the backdrop.

Finish painting your backdrop

Backdrop painting is much like scenery. It is never really finished, or is it? If the backdrop looks good at this point, stop. You can always go back and touch up the backdrop after the scenery is finished. In fact, I highly recommend it. The best way to get that backdrop to match the scenery, and vice versa, is to go back and blend the colors of the two. If you have put all the scenery in place, and the colors of some of the trees on the backdrop don't match the modeled ones, go in and make the changes on the backdrop. The backdrop can be reworked anytime. If the backdrop is too far to touch up, chances are that the changes wouldn't be all that visible; you might as well take that modeling time and focus it elsewhere. Just remember, even though acrylic paint dries permanent, there is nothing permanent about it because you can paint over it.

Using photos on a backdrop

You can use photographs on the backdrop very effectively. Cutting out only what you need of a photo and pasting it onto a backdrop of sky color eliminate many of the problems with this technique like blending and getting rid of that unsightly seam. Bill and Mary Miller have used several different photo murals on

The backdrop of this scene was painted first. After the scenery was finished, the backdrop was detailed and finished to match. This works well if the backdrop is in reach.

Helpful Hint #2 When your acrylic brushes wear out and start to become frayed and misformed, don't throw them out! You will find that the rough shapes of these brushes will work well for irregularly shaped subjects like trees, bushes, and clouds.

Bill Miller

C&S number 8 on a caboose hops under the airway between buildings of the Masters and Potter Boiler Works at Ruby on Bill and Mary Miller's On3 Ohio Creek Subdivision. The amount of depth the photo murals give the scene is astounding.

their layout with great success. They apply their technique to photo murals purchased commercially, but it will work with custom photos (your own photo blow-ups) too. Use an X-acto knife with a number 11 blade to carefully cut away the sky portion and any out-of-scale foreground features like buildings.

Bill uses a wallpapering technique when applying the mural to the backdrop. He draws a light tracing of the mural. He then applies wallpaper paste to the mural and the backdrop, following the instructions on the product. Then he positions the mural on the backdrop. The advantage of wallpaper paste is that it cleans up with a damp sponge and doesn't have any distracting sheen when dry.

Yet another technique that Bill uses to his advantage is layering murals. By using some murals that are lighter or faded toward the back, and laying on brighter or darker murals over the front, you can create the illusion of distance. Don't be afraid to use just portions or pieces of the photo murals to get the right effect. Hide the joints and seams with a tiny splash of acrylic paint mixed to match the mural. I think you'll be amazed at how quickly you can blend these unsightly seams away. In fact, combining these murals with a hand-painted backdrop will really trick the eye!

Chapter Five

Moving to the tabletop

Before you actually get to the scenicking stage, you need a foundation to work on. Real scenery is never flat, so even if your layout consists of a 4 x 8-foot sheet of plywood, some land forms are called for. Something to consider before you get too far is the importance of making the scenery drop below the level of your track. Prototype railroads purposely have their roadbeds high above watercourses and potentially flooded areas. And the scenery on your layout should also drop below the railhead. This is why many layouts are constructed with plywood or spline roadbed.

On the HO Alkali Central layout, plaster gauze was used for the sub-base of the scenery. It is easy to use and durable.

Above: Prototype railroad engineering follows the land and usually uses the "cut-and-fill" method of construction. Notice how this Southern Pacific train climbing the three percent grade of Colorado's Tennessee Pass hugs the mountain scenery. The train is crossing a fill over the Eagle River on a small culvert—not as dramatic as a curved trestle, but much more common.

By using plywood cut in this "cookie cutter" method, you not only save money by reducing the amount of plywood you have to purchase, but you also then have the ability to extend the scenery below and above track level, like the real thing. You can construct this sub-base scenery in several ways. I will go over the advantages and disadvantages of each.

Plaster gauze scenery sub-base

Using plaster gauze as a scenery base is a quick and easy way to get the land forms started. This material is the plaster-coated gauze mesh material com-monly used in the medical profession to set broken bones. Fortunately for us model rail-roaders, you don't need the pain of a broken limb to use this great material for scenery making. The material is now packaged under several brand names and is avail-able at many hobbyshops.

The first step in using this mate-rial as a sub-base for your scenery is to create some landforms. Two materials are commonly used for this purpose—window screening or cardboard strips supported with scraps of wood. If you use window screening, pick a syn-thetic material rather than metal. The last thing you want is rusting scenery. Lace the cardboard strips together and form them to the contours you want for your scenery. You can assemble both materials by using a staple gun or, even better, a hot-glue gun.

Form the scenery so that there are realistic drainage patterns away from the railroad. A look at the prototype can give you a wealth of ideas about sub-base construction. Many railroads used so-called "cut-and-fill" con-struction. To maintain a steady and low gradient, railroads relied on removing earth from high areas and using the same earth to fill in the ravines and such. This is actually harder to do effectively on a model, since you build the roadbed and track before the scenery. Sometimes the space restrictions of a model railroad limit the amount of prototype engineering you can copy.

Once you have constructed the scenery sub-base, it is time to cover it with the plaster gauze material. You simply cut the material into small sheets or strips, dip it into a bucket of water, and place it over the sub-base. Smaller pieces of the gauze are easier to handle. That is all there is to it. The scenery should start to take on the look of moun-tains or rolling hills, or whatever type of scenery you are modeling. One of the pluses of using this

Above: Before applying the plaster gauze, build up landforms with strips of cardboard or window screening. On his O scale layout, George Sebastian-Coleman made the landforms with chicken wire.

Above: Apply the plaster gauze material over the cardboard or screen sub-base. Overlap the pieces to give the gauze more strength.

Right: After the plaster gauze dries, give the resulting scenery sub-base a coat or two of plaster or Scuptamold.

Below: The sub-base of the scenery in this photo of the HOn3 Rio Grande at Durango was all constructed using Hydrocal-soaked paper towels. This type of scenery sub-base was more popular before the widespread availability of plaster gauze.

plaster gauze is how neat it is. There is no mixing and dripping. A disadvantage is the cost of the plaster gauze.

A similar technique is using Hydrocal-soaked paper towels. Hydrocal is a lightweight plaster-like material that is available at most hobby shops. Many home building centers sell it in bulk. You mix this material with water in small batches to the consistency of thick pea soup. Use heavy-duty paper towels (like the coarse brown type in those gas station restroom dispensers). Mix only small batches at a time, because Hydrocal dries extremely fast. Using Hydrocal is less expensive, especially when you buy it in bulk, but it is messier than plaster gauze.

After you finish the sub-base using either technique, it is time to coat the surface with a thin layer or two of plaster or Scuptamold. This gives the sub-base more strength, especially in the areas where more support may be necessary. At this point you can add rock castings if you wish (see next chapter). I also like to paint the entire surface of the scenery with a coat of the scenery base color. This will cover up the stark white raw plaster scenery and help you see how the landforms are taking shape. Changes are easy to make by simply removing the undesirable area and starting over. While the scenery base color is still wet, you

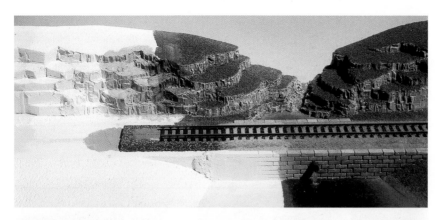

Left: Scenery builder Ron Hatch builds his scenery sub-base with insulation foam. One benefit of using this material is that rocks and other scenery foams can be carved directly into the sub-base. He used foam for the rock retaining wall and subroadbed of the railroad, showing how useful this material can be.

Above: A portion of Homer Henry's HO layout is shown in the very early stages of scenery construction. Homer is using a combination of plaster gauze and foam for the sub-base of the scenery. Feel free to use any combination of scenery methods to get the job done on your own layout.

can add scenery textures, such as ground foam, directly to it. A nice layer of ground foam will actually adhere to the paint, and it provides a great starting point to your scenery texture. By now it'll start to look like real scenery. You can add more texture materials later with an adhesive.

Insulation foam for the sub-base

Another material that is really picking up steam for use in scenery-making is household insulation foam. It is found at home building centers and is commonly blue or pink. it's available in 4 x 8-foot sheets of various thickness. Try several different thickness, and see what you are most comfortable using. The color doesn't matter; you'll just have to put up with it until you apply that coat of scenery base color. I commonly ask someone at the lumberyard to cut the 4 x 8-foot sheets in halves

or quarters for easy shipment home. You do get funny looks, though. "Are you sure you want these sheets cut in half?" someone is sure to ask. While you're at the lumberyard, ask if they have any damaged pieces. Many times you can get them for free. One thing to watch out for: be sure you don't use the foam material commonly used for insulated coolers. This material is beaded and is not suitable for scenery construction.

Using insulation foam is an excellent way to create the sub-base of your scenery. The material is not that expensive, and what I like about it is that you get to carve your scenery like a sculptor. First, you create a rough terrain by stacking layers of insulation foam where you want your scenery to be. You can assemble them with an adhesive like latex Liquid Nails or one especially

made for foam. You don't want an adhesive that will eat away the foam or one that doesn't stick to it. Ask for help at a home building center and they will point you to the right adhesive. I have used a hot-glue gun with some success. It does melt the surface of the foam, but you can use it if you work fast.

The next step is to carve these layers to represent land forms. A hot-wire tool will give a quick cut. I also use a serrated knife to carve the foam. You can even carve decent-looking rooks directly into the foam. Once you have the surface all roughed up and carved to represent rock, try giving it a coat of scenery base color. You'll be amazed at how well carved foam insulation represents rocks. For more rolling terrain, a Surform tool is great. One drawback to using insulation foam starts to rear its ugly head when you start carving or using the Surform. The process is really messy. And static electricity will make all the little pieces stick to everything. Keep a shop vacuum handy for cleanup. A bucket of water and a sponge are useful for getting rid of the static.

If you have ever taken a close look at a topographical map, you will have noticed all sorts of lines that show the elevation of the landforms. These lines trace the land at a certain elevation and are separated by a rise or fall in a specified number of feet. The closer the lines are, the faster the rise or fall is. What does all of this have to do with constructing scenery with insulation foam? Notice the similarity between the stacked-up sheets of insulation

foam when viewed from directly above and a topographic map. If you start thinking of each layer of foam as one of those lines, you'll soon be building up the land forms more quickly and without as much waste.

After forming and carving the insulation foam sub-base scenery, you will next patch all the cracks between layers. Use a material that adheres to foam. Companies such as Polyterrain and Woodland Scenics actually have a product for this purpose. I have had luck painting the foam with the latex scenery base color first, and then using a material that adheres to latex paint. The latex paint seems to adhere well to the foam, and many patching materials adhere to latex. Use a material that will accept some expansion and contraction. By painting the foam first, you will get a better idea of where the problem cracks are without all the distraction of that pretty blue or pink color. A coat of plaster or Sculptamold is also useful but not necessary.

Foam insulation was used between the scenery and the backdrop to hide the joint and provide a seamless transition between the two. Using both acrylic paints and scenery materials to finish this area further helped the illusion.

The biggest difference between using plaster gauze and insulation foam is the way you get to the finished scenery forms. With gauze, you build up the scenery. With foam, you actually carve the scenery to get to the final result. The gauze is faster, foam slower. The foam is lighter and somewhat stronger. If you are planning to "plant" hundreds of trees on the scenery, the foam will stay more integral. Poking holes with a toothpick for the tree is also quite easy in foam, while plaster requires more effort. It just depends on what you like to do, and what your type of scenery calls for. Try both, and see what you like better. You'll probably use both for different parts of the scenery.

Blending the sub-base with the backdrop

It is fun to trick the human eye in the area between the real scenery and the backdrop. Like the beautiful scenes we see at many city museums, the space between the scenery and the backdrop can make or break the believability of a scene.

One easy way to disguise this space is to simply make the hill closest to the backdrop drop away from the viewer. Another set of hills then rises up on the backdrop, and these are painted. There is no visible seam between the two to distract the eye.

Another way is to fill in the seam at the backdrop, using pieces of foam or plaster cloth. This technique is similar to curving a backdrop to hide a corner, only it is horizontal and on a much smaller scale. Then when you add scenery, bring it up and "feather" it onto the painted backdrop to disguise the seam. You'll find other ways to disguise the seam between the real scenery and the backdrop in Chapter 10.

Eric Brooman

Chapter • Six

Modeling rocks

Because gradients are and were so important to railroads, rights-of-way in many areas were blasted straight through rock. Even in the flattest parts of the nation, the cut-and-fill method was used in the hilly parts, unearthing visible rock formations along the right-of-way. No matter what part of the country you model, your layout could probably use some rocky areas.

Utah Belt GP60 3810 exits the shed at Tunnel 4 in the Flaming River Gorge at Iron Mountain, New Mexico. Eric Brooman made sure the rockwork on his layout simulated the rock in UB territory.

Top left: A pair of C&NW Dash-9s exit a tunnel portal surrounded by rocks made from insulation foam. When carved with simple tools such as an ordinary kitchen steak knife, this material works very well to simulate a rock surface.

Top right: More subtle rock effects can also be carved into the insulation. Use a combination of a serrated knife and Surform tool to get this rockwork.

Above: Stratified rocks can be carved into the surface of foam insulation. It takes a lot of horizontal carving to achieve the effect. Notice how coloring the foam makes a huge difference in the appearance of the finished rock.

Using carved insulation foam

One way to model rocks is to use the same material you used for the scenery sub-base. This blue or pink home insulation material can be carved into some very realistic-looking rocks. As I noted in Chapter 5, make sure you are not using the material commonly found in insulated coolers. This material is too beaded and doesn't work for rock carving.

I use a serrated steak or paring knife for most of my carving. A serrated knife is great for getting that rough-cut-rock look, which you want for most rock formations. Begin to rough up the surface of the foam with the knife. Cut and gouge the foam to start individualizing the rock formations. Follow photos of the prototype you are modeling to simulate the type of rock common to the area. Stratified rocks require more horizontal carving, while igneous rocks demand more random cut lines and gouges. A set of

chisels might be useful for carving the rocks as well. Use any tools you want to get the look you are after. I still find that the serrations of the steak knife do as good a job as any for getting that random rock look. Keep carving until the surface of the foam has lost all of its smoothness and manmade straight lines.

By now you are probably saying to yourself, "This 1!@$* foam rock doesn't look like real rocks at all!" Trust me; the next step will help out the situation. Painting the rocks with a coat of your scenery base color will make all of that carving come to life and

Right: Other types of rocks can be carved into foam. Use a picking and ripping motion with the edge of a steak knife. Certain types of carving blades also work well. Experiment on a scrap piece of foam to see how the tool performs.

will actually make it look more like rock. Don't forget to get the paint in all of the nooks and crannies so the foam color doesn't show through.

This coat of scenery base paint will also reveal any areas that need a little more carving to look more realistic. Just carve away at the rocks and then splash on some more base coat when you're finished. The foam is now ready for some staining and coloring, which is covered later in this chapter.

One benefit of constructing rocks with insulation foam is their light weight. They are perfect for any portable layout or one that you will move someday. These rocks are also inexpensive, since you don't need any other materials. The only bad thing about using foam for rockwork is the mess of those foam shavings. Keep a shop vacuum handy, and the mess will be controllable.

Using plaster and rubber molds for rocks

A proven way to construct rocks is with molding plaster and rubber molds. A great number of different rock molds are available commercially. Try to buy the ones with the greatest detail and largest variety.

Begin by wetting the molds with a mixture of water and a few drops of a wetting agent like liquid dish soap. This allows the plaster to flow into all the details of the casting. Shake the molds to remove any excess water. Next, mix the molding plaster in a small bucket, using roughly two parts plaster to one part water. Make sure you stir the plaster gently to avoid getting too many bubbles in the mix. The bubbles will rear their ugly heads

when the mold is removed, looking like miniature craters. Pour this mixture into the molds. Feel free to vary the amount of plaster you pour into each mold. The different thicknesses of the castings will come in handy when it is time to position them onto the layout.

Carefully remove the castings once the plaster has set, put them on the layout where they are needed. Place them randomly like pieces of a puzzle. This "dry" fit will help locate the best places for each casting. Keep the castings as close together as possible if you're covering a large area. This helps to disguise the individual molds.

I like to use more plaster to attach the castings in place. Spray the area to be covered with water. This improves the adhesion of the castings to the scenery. Next, cover the area with a soupy mix of plaster and water, slightly thicker than the casting mixture. Mist the rear of the castings with water and then press them in place. As you position the larger castings, you might find that breaking several of them into smaller pieces will help. While the plaster is somewhat soft, carve the areas between the castings and use a knife to blend them together.

All of those little scraps and pieces of plaster that accumulate when you're casting plaster rocks can be used too. And save the plaster molds that don't turn out.

Molding plaster and rock molds are two staples for casting rocks. Both are readily available at most hobby shops. A scenery catalog will offer a wealth of different rubber rock molds.

Break this scrap plaster into random small pieces and use it as riprap on the layout. Real railroads always use riprap and rock to shore up their rights-of-way.

Color this scrap plaster using the same scenery base paint as you used on the rest of the scenery before gluing it to the scenery. Just make sure to cover the white areas, or the scrap will look like bits of broken plaster on the layout.

Casting a special batch of plaster specially tinted with powdered pigments to match the scenery works even better. I break up this plaster with a hammer into the sizes I want. The color is throughout the plaster, so there are none of those annoying white chunks of raw plaster showing up over time. Use the riprap wherever appropriate on the layout, such as behind retaining walls or along the fills of the roadbed.

George Sebastian-Coleman

George Sebastian-Coleman

Top left: A plaster casting representing the Palisades section of George Sebastian-Coleman's South Park layout is installed after dry-fitting.

Top right: More plaster is now installed below the Palisades wall. Note the test of some stains on the Palisade wall and how they dramatically change the look of the plaster casting.

This scene uses pre-cast plaster castings, fitted in place on the layout. Fit them as close together as possible and fill in the gaps with more plaster to disguise the individual molds.

Casting rocks in place on the layout

In this method you place the setting rock castings directly onto the scenery. Since you form the castings in place, the molds conform better to the scenery shapes. By overlapping the molds as you go along, you can eliminate some of the recognizable look of the molds. Anything you can do to disguise the shape and sizes of the molds will help.

Thoroughly wet the area of scenery to be covered by the molds. Now wet the molds and pour the mix of two parts plaster, one part water into the molds. Let the molds cure long enough

so the plaster doesn't pour from the mold. The molds should still be flexible.

Now place them on the scenery where you want them. Make sure all edges are securely flush with the scenery. Hold them firmly in place for at least 5 to 10 minutes, or until the molds become warm and the plaster underneath them becomes inflexible. Now carefully pull the mold away. Clean up the plaster that leaked from the edges and blend it between the molds. Repeat these steps with different molds, or the same mold, rotated in position, until the area you want covered is complete.

Coloring rock

Once the rock areas are finished and colored with the scenery base paint, it's time to give the rocks some life with color and stain. I like to use a base coat, even on the molded castings, to eliminate those unnatural specks of white that often appear. This base coat gives a nice color to start with. Begin by studying different color photos of the area you are modeling. Note the different tones in the rock, and pick the acrylic colors you think you will need. I like to mix all of the different acrylic paints with white to see what different color tones appear.

You can stain rocks with

Top left: Use scrap plaster or plaster that you tint first and then break into pieces as riprap around retaining walls and the right-of-way. This scene shows some of these bits of plaster among a retaining wall on the On30 Elk Mountain Timber Company Railroad by Bill and Mary Miller. Note how the foreground scenery blends perfectly with the backdrop and the amount of depth it provides.

Top right: A view of a Southern Pacific eastbound freight traversing the Royal Gorge shows several different tones in the rocks. The browns predominate, but lighter reds and even a blackish color are visible. Don't forget to include some greens to represent moss and small plants growing among the rocks.

Coloring the rockwork with acrylics is easy. Note the steps shown in this photo of the raw foam, scenery base paint, rock coloring, and ground textures. Give the rocks some highlights by drybrushing a lighter tone over the rock color.

thinned acrylics. Thin the different acrylic colors in a plastic lid from an ice cream pail, or something similar. Wash the colors over the rocks with a fairly large brush. If you use too much paint, the color will appear too dark. The paint should flow into all of the minute cracks and detail of the rocks. Add some titanium white acrylic paint

to the stains mixed on the palette for different color tones.

A thin mix of black acrylic paint misted onto the rock castings will also accent detail. A small amount goes a long way. Thinned yellows and browns will warm up the color tone on the rocks, while grays and blues will cool them down. Vary the colors by what kind of rocks are visible. Colors in an area of man-made excavation will be lighter and cleaner.

After the stain has dried, dry-

brushing lighter colors over the rocks will make them come alive. Dip an old brush into a color lighter than your rocks. Scrub off most of the paint on scrap cardboard. Drybrush the rock faces lightly, just hitting the high points of the rocks. The amount of detail this picks out is amazing. It also brings out flaws in the rock textures, so you may have to spruce up these areas later. Rocks come in all different colors and tones, so don't be afraid of some variety.

Chapter Seven

Ground textures

Adding ground texture to your landscape can bring a layout to life (almost literally, since ground foam and other materials represent live plants). Here's how to successfully use ground foam, and even lichen, on a model railroad.

Narrow Gauge 2-8-0 number 268 steams over a small wooden trestle on the outskirts of Durango, Colorado. All of the ground cover in this scene is ground foam. This is a dryer part of the country, so the ground cover is more burnt and brown than it is green.

Wayne Reid

This scene of a Pennsylvania express local cruising westbound under Flag Road bridge has incredible life because of the beautiful ground textures developed by Bill and Wayne Reid.

Using ground foam

One of the most popular ground textures is ground foam. There are many good ground foams available commercially, and they are not that expensive in the grand scheme of things. They come in many different colors and degrees of coarseness. I did something a little unusual before scenicking my layout (this may not be for everyone). I picked out a brand of ground foam and bought one bag of each color and coarseness in the entire line. This was a lot of bags of ground foam. Then I used old spaghetti sauce jars and the like, and put the different types of ground foam in each one. I also marked each bottle with the color and coarseness it contained. Wouldn't you know it, I used every color and coarseness, even on a small layout. Some colors you use much more than others. But I found that having all of them gave the scenery the

Above: A Conrail freight exits the tunnel at Gallitzin, Pennsylvania. The incredible variety of ground cover and bushes is readily visible in this autumn scene. This variety of textures is what we strive for in our miniature layout scenes.

Helpful Hint #1 Buy a quart of matte medium at your local hobby or art store. It costs quite a bit, but it will go a long way on the model railroad. A plastic one-gallon milk container (after you have finished with the contents) is great as a storage container. Pour in the quart of matte medium, add a teaspoon of soap or two, and top off with water. You now have a gallon mixture of matte medium diluted 3 to 1. This should last a while. Don't shake or stir the jug when using it. Let the particulates that you don't need gather on the bottom where they belong.

Wayne Reid

Above: All the ground cover on the *Model Railroader* staff project layout of the Alkali Central is ground foam. Note the coarser ground foam representing larger bushes scattered at the base of the stock pens.

A Western Maryland local traverses a scene with plenty of green ground cover, more typical of the eastern United States. The amount of ground cover can define what part of the country is modeled, even before the train shows up, giving it away.

scenic variety of the real thing. Just don't overdo it with the bright, gaudy colors. They look best in the garden next to that old house. Having the bottles marked makes it easier to note which color or variety is running low so you can buy more before you run out.

You can add ground foam at two different stages. First, you can put it directly onto the surface of the scenery right after you paint the surface with your chosen base color. An advantage of doing it this way is that it's fast. One minute your scenery is all white plaster or blue foam, and the next it is a nice earthy color with grasses and other foliage. You can always go back and add more later. In fact, you probably should, since not all of the coarser foams will adhere to the base paint.

You should use another method if you are staining the rocks and groundwork. Since a stain or wash has no adhesive value, you must add ground foam after the stain is dry. Use a diluted mixture of white glue or acrylic matte medium to bond the ground foam to the scenery.

Even though it is tempting, resist the urge to use real dirt collected from the area that is being modeled. Even if it is cleaned and

sifted, it can still have small metal particles in it, and these don't mix well with the magnets on the motors of our favorite locomotives. Even if you take all the precautions, the colors of the dirt taken from the prototype won't look right under typical layout conditions. No layout lighting is as bright as the sun, so all material gathered from outside will appear darker. It is better to use earth-colored ground foams. Try to match the colors to photos of the particular prototype viewed under the layout lighting.

More on matte medium

When gluing scenic materials such as ground foam and ballast, a material called matte medium works well. Matte medium is available at any art store and many hobby shops. It is about the consistency of white glue, but you don't use it in that form for model railroad scenery. Thin it 3 or 4 parts water to one part matte medium. Mix in a wetting agent, such as a teaspoon or so of liquid detergent, as well. Apply this solution to scenery as a bonding agent.

First arrange the scenery materials the way you want then on the layout. Then, using a spray bottle (I use an old rinsed-out glass cleaner bottle), carefully wet

the area to be bonded. Use water with a couple drops of liquid dish soap as the wetting agent. Then apply the solution of matte medium, using anything from an eyedropper to a spoon. I like to use an empty white glue bottle for applying the matte medium. This type of bottle works well because you can adjust the flow of the matte medium.

After applying the matte medium solution, the scenery usually looks kind of rough— somewhat dark and shiny. It's really hard to tell how the scenery will turn out. Don't despair; just leave the scenery alone, even though it is tempting to "cultivate" the scenery some more. After allowing the proper drying time, things will start to look a lot better. Check the drying process the next day. You might find a few areas that need another application of matte medium. This is common, especially with track ballast, or areas that contain a lot of glued material.

Another somewhat less expensive adhesive is white glue. Thin it and apply it in the same manner. Its only drawback is that it sometimes dries with more sheen than matte medium. Also, it doesn't seem to mix as well, and small white flecks of glue sometimes appear in the finished

A Union Pacific streamliner whizzes past the section crew getting ready for a day's work. The ground foam in the eroded areas of the hillside needed several applications of matte medium before everything was solidly glued in place.

scenery. But the price is right and in a pinch, the white glue works just fine.

Sprucing up lichen

For many years, before the introduction of the many textures and colors of ground foam, there was lichen. Lichen was about the best thing you could use to represent ground cover, bushes, and even trees. Most of the lichen you get in a bag is unusable as is. Only the finely textured tip pieces work best unmodified. But the rest of the lichen can still be a great material for your scenery. It just needs a little pick-me-up.

Lichen is great as a "skeleton" for your up-close bushes and trees. Even those coarse-looking leftover pieces look good this way. Add different shades of ground foam to any subtle green or even brown lichen. The lichen takes on the role of branches, and the ground foam represents the leaves. Use a spray glue such as 3M Photo Mount or even, believe it or not, hair spray. You want a glue that eventually loses

Helpful Hint #1 When arranging bushes and ground cover, make sure it they are randomly, and not evenly, spaced. There are a few areas where the shrubs and bushes are spaced out, but they are not typical. Abo Canyon on Santa Fe's Belen Cutoff main line through New Mexico is a good example. Notice how all of the bushes are evenly spaced out on the mountains. If this is the prototype you're modeling, then you'll arrange the ground cover like this. But generally speaking, random arrangements of bushes and ground cover look much better.

The almost unreal arrangement of shrubs on the mountains of Abo Canyon, New Mexico, is not very typical. Random and grouped arrangements usually look better.

its tackiness so it doesn't become a dust magnet. Test several different products to see what works best for you. If you go with hairspray, choose an unscented brand, unless you want the layout to smell like a beauty salon.

For distant trees and bushes, adding a small amount of ground foam on top is all you need to make lichen look very convincing. Remember, the farther back a scenic feature is, the less detailed it has to (or even should) be. Large groups of lichen look best. If you are modeling parts of the East and Midwest, covering the entire hillsides with lichen forests will look great. Just be careful about how much lichen you use unmodified. If the lichen starts to look too coarse, it's best to perk it up with some ground foam. Some parts of the west have bushes and trees that are very coarse in nature. The rough-looking qualities of lichen are perfect for modeling these types of foliage.

Allen McClelland has always used lichen in some form on his Virginian & Ohio layout. As lichen ages, it gets more and more brittle and dull. A half-and-half mixture of glycerine (used in flower preservation) and rubbing alcohol spray-misted onto old lichen will rejuvenate it nicely. Just be very careful of the overspray; use plenty of cardboard or other materials to mask off the area that doesn't need the spray. Allen has lichen on his layout that is almost 40 years old and is still surviving. He has revitalized much of that old lichen with a nice dose of ground foam and matte medium. But his layout does prove that something organic such as lichen can last an incredibly long time.

Eric Brooman

Summit siding in Flaming River Gorge on Eric Brooman's Utah Belt hosts a meet between trains. The edge of the river is home to plenty of lichen foliage because of the close proximity of a water supply.

Permanent snow scenes

Adding a snow scene to part of a layout can be a neat effect. Perhaps the railroad goes over a pass, making this area a perfect location for a snow scene. Snow can be a type of ground texture, so it is included in this chapter.

First, apply all the trees, rock, and ground textures that will be snow-covered. Unless the snow is incredibly deep, some of this scenery will show through in spots. And snow doesn't generally stick to near-vertical surfaces such as rock walls.

Then, after all of the scenery is installed and dry, sift molding plaster (Hydrocal can be used as well) over the scene with an old fine-mesh kitchen strainer. It will be snowing plaster! After sifting a light coat on everything, lightly mist everything to wet the plaster, using a spray bottle filled with water and a drop or two of dish soap. Too much water will make the plaster run. Apply just enough to saturate the plaster. Be sure to use a spray bottle with a very fine misting action to keep the plaster from moving too much. Let this dry thoroughly. Sift on more plaster and repeat the misting of water until the "snow" begins to accumulate. Keep repeating until you get the depth you want.

Be careful when applying the snow to the track areas. Make sure that the turnouts are cleaned out and the flangeways have proper clearance. Also, be careful around wood. Too much water on wood structures and other scenery can cause warping.

Notice how nicely the plaster snow sticks to pine trees and rock areas. Don't forget to plow the roads so the railroaders can get to work!

Chapter • Eight

Trees

Unless you model parts of the desert Southwest, or the Dakotas, you will need lots and lots of trees. Most areas that are interesting to model will require some. And fortunately for us modelers, many very nice trees are available right from the shelves of the hobby store. Some of these are ready-made, while others are kits. And many are so good they deserve up-front placement on the layout.

Pennsylvania Railroad cabin 477829 trails train CL-3, the Winchester Turn, on its way to Winchester, Virginia, on Bill and Wayne Reid's N scale layout. Clusters of beautiful trees towering over the train and structures gives the scene a definite eastern feel. Notice the lighter, bluer trees painted on the backdrop, and how they give the scene depth.

Wayne Reid

Hundreds of commercial trees and kits are available for good-looking models. Check out the incredible variety at a local hobby shop, or flip through the Walthers catalog. The aspens are from a weed material called Forest in a Flash, available from Jane's Trains.

This mountaintop is covered with trees made from craft store and natural materials. The pine trees are made from Bumpy Chenille; this material is less expensive than some of the commercial trees.

It's possible to make a realistic forest using a combination of commercial materials like these, homemade materials, and ground cover.

Most layouts will never have enough trees because of the cost and the time it takes to build that many trees. There are several ways to combine commercial materials with homemade or natural materials to make large quantities of more-affordable trees. If you are ever looking for a quick modeling project, adding a few trees won't hurt the layout.

Realistic pine trees

Anyone who models railroads in parts of the western U.S. and Canada will face a dilemma when it comes to covering the mountainsides with evergreens. Some of the store-bought varieties look great, but are way too expensive to use throughout the background, and are more suited as foreground models. The solution of using Bumpy Chenille for pine trees has been used for years. But unless you have been to a craft store to buy some, you probably don't know what it looks like. The material is similar to a huge, overgrown pipe cleaner with growths every few inches. It is available at any

length, and with different-size bumps. I have found that the most useful size bumps are the 3- and 4-inch size. They come in many different gaudy colors. Buy dark brown, since you will paint them green, anyway. After you paint the trees green, if some of the brown shows through it will look like the branches of the tree. The secret to making these trees look realistic is proper grooming and painting.

The trees are easy enough that you can make a batch while watching football on television. Just be careful with the scissors when your team makes a touchdown. Begin by cutting the bumps apart. Don't use your wife's favorite sewing scissors either—the wire in the Bumpy Chenille isn't kind to a good pair of scissors. Now trim the bump to the height of tree you want. Remember to vary your tree heights. I trim some of the chenille material away at the base, making it easier to "plant" the trees. Next, rough up the shape of the tree with scissors while rotating it horizontally. This gives the illusion of individual branches and gives the tree a more natural look. I trim some of the material at the top to give the tree a more pointed top. Some of these trees can also be

Bumpy Chenille comes in different colors and sizes, measured by the size of the bumps. I use brown, since I paint them green to cover the sheen of the material.

Cut the bumps apart at the thinnest area between bumps. Each bump will make two trees of various sizes or one larger tree.

Cut the bumps in half, varying the size for different-size trees. Even the very smallest tree is useful as a distant tree on the mountaintops.

Remove some material from the base of the tree for ease of planting. On some of the larger trees, remove enough material to represent the trunk.

Rough up the chenille material with scissors to give the tree a better shape. Don't forget to make the tops of the trees pointed.

The Bumpy Chenille pine trees are now finished and ready for painting. Before you know it, you'll have a forest of these little trees.

trimmed with a trunk. Just trim more of the chenille material away. The trees are now finished and ready for painting. Plant all your nicely groomed, but still shiny, brown trees about an inch or so apart on a piece of scrap insulation foam.

Now comes the painting part. Use the cheapest flat dark green matte spray paint you can find. The nicest I have found is at the same craft store I buy my Bumpy Chenille. It is Country Colors by Accent. The main color I use is 378 Pine Needle Green (surprise, surprise). The trees will look even more realistic if you vary the color a little. Some of the other colors I use are 135 Verdi Green, 387 Village Green, 379 Telemark Green, 138 Sweet Chocolate, and 380 Wicker. I use all these colors for tinting after I have painted the trees with the base color of Pine Needle Green. The two brown colors are great for tinting some

of them to represent dead or dying trees. Don't be afraid of over-painting these trees. I painted some batches so heavily that the paint started to bead on the tiny chenille strands. It dried and looked like clumps of pine needles on the ends of branches.

The trees that are trimmed to have a trunk are now all green. I use brown acrylic paint straight out of the tube to paint the trunks. (Raw and burnt umber work well.) Again, just slop the paint on. Heavier paint will disguise the pipe cleaner-look of the trunks.

Now comes the fun part—planting the trees on your layout.

The trees look great in thick clumps, with occasional trees spread out. Put the smaller trees toward the backdrop to represent more distant trees. Also put the lighter green trees farther back. The trees with the trunks are obviously planted closer up. You didn't trim and paint a trunk for nothing. Always vary the sizes of the trees and the shapes of the groupings. Before you know it, that whole bunch of trees you made will be swallowed up by your scenery, and you'll be grabbing the scissors and spray paint, and watching another football game.

> **Helpful Hint #1** Try using a dark green or even black spray paint and lightly mist the underside of your tree. Spray directly parallel to the trunk of the tree at the bottom of the foliage. This will give the tree more depth, and some of the leaves and branches will appear to be in shadow. Don't overdo it—a light misting will suffice. Use the same technique with lighter colors misted from above to represent highlights.

Top left: Look at the variety of tree shapes visible in this scene along the Wisconsin Central at Theresa Station, Wisconsin. Notice how many don't have visible trunks. You can model this effect using the commercial foliage materials in clump form. Also note how some of the trees loom large over the *Nebraska Zephyr* trainset.

Top right: Don't forget to include a few detailed, gnarled foreground trees similar to this one along the BNSF at West Marietta, South Dakota.

Left: Trees look best when clustered in groups. The occasional loner is fine, but just as in real life, if there is one, there are usually more nearby.

Deciduous trees

Besides the hundreds of good-looking deciduous trees available commercially, there are ways to make them with natural materials. You will still need to buy packages of the foliage material, but the trunk of the tree comes from the great outdoors.

The next time you are out camping, trainwatching, or finding yourself outdoors, think small trees. Many trees and shrubs have young branches that are usable for the trunks of model trees. Look for fine bark structure and a large number of branches. When trimmed, these real tree branches make great trunks. Since the ends of the tree branches don't have the fine, lacy branches of real trees, they will have to be disguised. Make sure the tips of these tree structures are covered with foliage material to hide the ends. In no time you will have a good-looking tree. These may not be good enough for foreground models, but they're great scattered in the middle and background.

Certain real weeds make good trees too. The only problem is that they have to be preserved and colored to look right. Experiment with them to see if they can stand the rigors of time on a layout. Some very nice commercial trees are actually made from natural weeds. Since someone else has gone through all of the time involved in preserving and coloring, I recommend going this route for these trees.

Top left: A set of BN SD60MAC's heads north along the Soo Line's main at Bellevue, Iowa. This is a typical autumn scene with green and dried grasses, and subtly colored trees. Most trees in a fall color scene should be more muted in color.

Top right: Horse Shoe Curve on a beautiful October 23, 1988. This was a rare year in which color at its peak was incredibly vivid. Not every year looks like this. Weather, wind, and other factors prevent it.

Right: Eric Brooman modeled these aspen trees with fine trunk structures gathered from the great outdoors. Always keep on the lookout for natural scenery materials.

Eric Brooman

Autumn foliage

Modeling the beauty of autumn is something that crosses every modeler's mind. The incredible red maples of Vermont, or golden, quaking leaves of aspens in the Rockies are great inspirations.

Fall colors on a layout can be beautiful. Just be careful with the bright colors—believability of the model is at stake. That brilliant red maple you see in real life is hard enough to believe. This same tree in model form will be even harder, unless it is surrounded by a believable environment.

Most trees don't turn the incredible colors we are all so familiar with. They are subtle shades of yellow, orange, red, and brown. Some years are better for fall color than others, and it seems that there are more years with average-to-below-average color. If the year is a good one for color, enjoy it while you can. If you photograph real railroads, you will notice how hard it is to get bright autumn trees in the shot. This isn't to say you shouldn't model fall color, just be careful how you do it.

Chapter • Nine

Water

No matter what type of scenery you will have on your layout, chances are you will need some modeled water. When surveyors of the railroad builders searched for the preferred routes, the best route often followed a water course because of the necessity of low grades. Many routes follow rivers, creeks, or edges of bodies of water. Besides, having water on the layout makes everything else about your scenery more believable.

A Union Pacific freight with C&NW and SP power passes by Spectacle Lake. Modeling water can be a daunting task, but several methods make it easier for a layout to get the "wet look."

Left: Four Rio Grande F units rumble along a small creek in the Rockies.

Below left: A westbound Southern Pacific freight on the Royal Gorge Route closely follows the Arkansas River at Granite, Colorado. Notice how dark the water appears, with some blue tints reflected from the sky above.

Bottom left: Skilled scenery builder Ron Hatch built this section of water using a foam base. The water area is completely flat, but the way it is painted gives the illusion of depth. Stippling also gives the gloss medium a wavy look.

Which type of scenery you decide to model will have a large effect on what type of water you will require. Obviously, certain parts of the country have more water than others. Lakes, ponds, creeks, rivers, and even the ocean can be successfully modeled. One thing to keep in mind is that all scenery is shaped by the incredible forces of time and water. Water has played a big part in the shape of all the scenery as we know it. For example, most canyons have been formed by the erosion of water over many years. So if there is a canyon on your layout, there should probably be water at the bottom in the form of a river or creek. Take a good look at the area you are modeling, and you'll probably find more water than you realized.

Modeling water is easier than you might think. There are several ways to get to the final effect, and as usual some are easier than others. First, I will explain how acrylic gloss medium works for almost all situations. Then I'll cover the two-part-resin method for modeling water. Enough said—it's time to dive in!

Building a water base

No matter what method you will use for modeling water, you will need a level base for the water surface. All calm water surfaces such as lakes and ponds

Top left and right: Stippling the paint as the lake bed is blended provides a nice rippled surface for the gloss medium. Note the faint reflection of the train and scenery. Compare this to the water in this prototype photo of a Santa Fe westbound passing a small pond west of Leeds, Illinois.

must be perfectly flat. Get that old level out and make sure that the surface you build for the water is level. Rivers are mostly level too, but they do flow downstream, so a slight tilt downward is okay for them. The most obvious way to make a base is to install a sheet of wood or plywood at the proper level for water. Keep the water level well below the track level and away from roads and structures, unless of course you want possible miniature floods in spring. How far below depends on the terrain and the type of scenery the railroad runs through. The scenery can then be built to the edge of the lake or river.

Wayne Reid

Above: A Reading pool coal train is eastbound at Green Mountain Curve and about to cross a small stream. Bill and Wayne Reid used casting resin for this river on their N scale layout.

Modeling water with acrylic gloss medium

Using acrylic gloss medium is one of the more satisfying ways to create realistic modeled water without fuss. Gloss medium is essentially an acrylic paint that dries clear and glossy. With a convincing base, it looks great as modeled water. Gloss medium has several advantages: there is no mixing of resins and no smell; it dries quickly; and it really does

stand up well. If you make a mistake, you can start over and repaint and regloss the surface of the water. At least give modeling water with gloss medium a try with a small water project. I think you'll be convinced.

Once you build the scenery to the water's edge, you can color it and the bottom of the water area with your scenery base color. Just make sure you don't get any of the actual scenery materials such as ground foam below the waterline.

The scenery base color works well for the areas right along the banks, but you need to give the illusion of depth to the water. Now comes the fun part, coloring the bottom of the lake. Notice that when you view real water surfaces, they appear quite dark. Use the scenery base color as a starting point, and begin to add darker colors of brown, blue, green, and black and blend them into the scenery base color. Acrylics dry fast, so try to work quickly. The deepest part of

Note the river's edge in this photo of a BN train along the Mississippi. The scenery along the water's edge is wet from wave action and is much darker.

This lake was originally poured with casting resin. That reflected the top edge of the backdrop. A new stippled surface coated with gloss medium gave the water a rippled surface.

the water will be the darkest. Try to refrain from using too much blue. The color of the water bottom or the water itself is not blue. What we perceive to be "blue" water is actually the reflection of the sky above. If all goes well, the gloss medium will reflect some of the blue backdrop on the layout for the same effect.

The blending of the dark colors on the water bottom doesn't have to be perfect, but the more feathered the blend is, the more it will give you the illusion of depth. If you are trying to model the rippled surface of a lake, one effect that goes a long way is stippling the paint as you blend. If you stipple the paint, there will be no need to stipple the gloss medium to create the same effect, and you avoid creating bubbles. Experiment on a scrap piece of cardboard with these effects and you'll be amazed. It really isn't that tough. I have had success blending these colors with my normal backdrop painting brushes.

An airbrush for this effect also works well. Just make sure that you use a tip and needle in your airbrush suited for the application of acrylic paints. You obviously won't be able to use the stippling technique for the ripples if you use an airbrush. Try stippling the scenery base color during its application, before you use the airbrush for blending the darker colors.

Applying the gloss medium

Once you are satisfied with the look of the water bottom, it is time to give it the "wet look." Applying gloss medium is similar to applying varnish on furniture, and some of the same rules apply. Brush slowly so you don't get lots of bubbles. Don't overbrush any one area, or you may get brush strokes or cloudiness. Apply gloss medium in thin coats, since heavy coats can crack. You can build up many thin coats to get the effect you are after.

You can stipple gloss medium to represent ripples, but watch out for the buildup of bubbles in the gloss medium. This also works well for representing a boiling surf or waves. Since the materials are so cheap, have some fun experimenting with gloss medium. You will probably be surprised at how easy it is to model good-looking water with this medium.

Modeling water with a two-part resin

Using a two-part resin for water areas is slightly different. You will still need a perfectly flat surface for the base of the water. But the illusion of depth is real, because the resin will have thickness. There are several different types of two-part resins, and some are downright dangerous because of the fumes. I once built a layout with a canyon that needed a river. I used plywood for the base and

built a nice-looking streambed with all of the detail. The scenery was built up along the edges. (This is important, as two-part resins are self-leveling.) I don't remember what type of two-part resin it was, but did it have an awful (and dangerous) smell! The water turned out all right, especially that huge pool on the floor, from the tiny leak in the plaster riverbed. Lesson learned—don't use the really bad-smelling resins, and make sure that your scenery doesn't have a leak!

But not all two-part resins are so nasty to use. A product called EnviroTex came out years after my experience. It does not have that terrible smell, but should still be used in a well-ventilated area, following all of the manufacturer's directions.

Build a riverbed and add all of the details that you want to show through the water. Rocks, fallen trees, even man-made items like tires or old cars tossed in the river. Make sure everything is in place and where you want it. This is important, since once you pour the casting resin, you can't make changes.

Even though EnviroTex is made to be poured in a thick layer, several thin layers will work better. There will be less chance of its cracking while it is setting up. EnviroTex sets up in several hours but takes at least three days to

A Rio Grande caboose passes a raft floating down a stream created with acrylics and gloss medium. It took many brushed-on coats of gloss medium to achieve the desired look.

The bridge over Rush Run hosts the local CL-7 on the Reid brothers' layout. Don't forget to add a couple of fishermen stalking their quarry along the riverbanks.

cure fully. Refrain from touching the resin to see how it is drying, even if the temptation is great.

EnviroTex dries to a mirror-like surface and represents a calm water surface very convincingly. It will reflect anything behind it perfectly. I actually found this to be a problem on one of my layouts. The top edge of the backdrop on this layout was only 27 inches high. So when you looked at the lake from most angles, you could see the top end of the backdrop and the stark white wall behind it. I had to fix the problem by repainting the resin surface of the lake with stippled acrylics and gloss medium to get the effect I was after. The rougher surface of the rippled gloss medium solved the reflection problems.

Rivers and rapids

You can model a river in much the same way as a lake. I like to use acrylic gloss medium applied over a river bottom. Detail this river bottom as much as you like, or just rely on the illusion of depth using acrylic paints applied the same way as on a larger body of water. You can add rocks made of plaster castings to the riverbed, or any other materials you want showing through the water. Just make sure that items such as rocks are smooth. Anything found in a river would be eroded. Then simply brush on several thin coats of acrylic gloss medium to represent the water.

You can also model a river by pouring casting resin into a stream bed. Several pours will probably be necessary, since the resin settles to the lowest points as it cures, sometimes leaving the higher points of the river dry. You can mix pigments into the resin to tint the water. In whitewater areas you could use white pigment, but a little bit goes a long way. Or you could drybrush a gloss white paint onto the casting resin surface after the resin is thoroughly dry. Or you could pour more casting resin over the white for a three-dimensional look.

One material I find helpful in modeling the rapids of rivers or a wavy lake is called Extra Heavy Gel Gloss. This is essentially a super-thick version of gloss medium. It is great for forming waves and rapids. Any texture that you brush on, such as stippling, tends to be more pronounced since this product is so much thicker. I have tried using a clear silicone caulking for rough-water areas. It looks great when you first apply it. But as time goes on, it gets very dull and starts to peel (sounds just like what it does when used for weather stripping, doesn't it).

Once the gloss medium or gel is dry it is time to add some frothing, foaming whitewater. Using white acrylic paint, drybrush some of the water around obstacles in the water. Rocks, trees, or whatever causes interference with the flow of water are all good places for a little whitewater. Just tickling the surface of the water with the drybrush seems to work best. Since the white acrylics dry somewhat flat in finish, another thin coat of gloss medium will finish it off. Now it's time to let those river rafters downstream!

Modeling the ocean

The best way to model the immensity of the ocean is to model just a part of it. If the ocean is to be in the foreground, nearer to the aisles, you can model it in the same way as a lake. But the ocean has unique attributes, chiefly waves and surf. Model them by using the gloss medium and Extra Heavy Gel Gloss, topped off with a little drybrushing with white acrylic. Look at photos of the ocean and you can see a very rhythmic flow to the surf. Use these photos as a guide to best capture that wave action.

The easiest way to represent the ocean is to have it completely painted on the backdrop. Just make sure to keep it completely level. Bring your scenery to the back edge of the backdrop, making sure that the seam between the modeled scenery and the backdrop doesn't show.

Chapter Ten

Blending scenery

One of the neatest effects you can see at a good public museum is the way the three-dimensional part of a display blends right into the painted backdrop. The best way to do this is to hide the joint between the scenery and the backdrop as much as possible. (This applies to a model railroad too.) There are several ways to blend the space between the scenery sub-base and the backdrop.

Rio Grande 484 pulls a stock train toward the pens at Durango, Colorado. Because of the close proximity of the track to the backdrop, all of the mountain scenery was painted on the backdrop and blended to match the foreground.

This view of the Alkali Central shows the real scenery butting directly onto the backdrop. This edge is treated like the tops of some hills, and matching acrylic paints carry some slightly farther hills into the background. As long as the colors match reasonably well, the seam will not be distracting.

Helpful Hint #1 What if you need preserve access to an area behind the layout, but still want to have a painted backdrop? Try what the Reid brothers have done on their N scale layout. They disguised some electrical outlets on the wall with a continuation of Green Mountain. They painted the rest of Green Mountain with matching paints. This allowed access to the utility, but the scene wasn't as broken up as if they had used just the scenery. Backdrop painting can be a great way not only to carry your scenery into the distance, but also to get around a necessary utility.

Wayne Reid

backdrop and the three-dimensional layout is by bringing the foreground scenery right up to the backdrop so it literally touches or attaches to it. By using acrylic paints on both the backdrop and the foreground scenery, you can "feather" them together for a seamless look. Ground textures sprinkled on the scenery, as well as onto the backdrop, work well also.

Using foliage for the blending

Another great way to disguise the gap is with foliage. Model trees, with one flat side, can be positioned right up against the backdrop. For a forested look, paint trees on the backdrop. Glue some of the foliage material to the real trees to blend the scene together.

Using acrylic paints on the scenery near the backdrop works well; likewise, attaching foliage and ground foam to the backdrop

Making it easier to blend

The easiest way is to let the hill or landform drop away before it gets to the backdrop. You can let the scenery butt up to the backdrop, but it will require more blending. Either way, color is the most important factor in getting the two blended. This is why I use the same scenery base color on both the actual scenery and the backdrop.

One of the most effective ways to hide the seam between the

Eric Brooman

Eric Brooman

Top left: A combination of commercial city backdrops and building flats created this urban scene on Eric Brooman's Utah Belt. Notice how Eric gave some buildings more relief to further enhance the illusion.

Top right: A prototype view of a Burlington Northern SD60M on a CP train through Milwaukee shows what appears to be building flats in the background. Constructing a scene like this with building flats allows more room on the layout for track and scenic details like the trees. Don't forget to add trees that are bigger than the trains in certain scenes too.

Above: In the background of this view of Durango, all buildings except the depot are cardboard cutouts done with color pencils. This technique works well for buildings if the layout is somewhat wide so the lack of detail is not noticed.

is a good technique. Blending (or feathering) all of these materials results in seams that are practically invisible.

Building flats

If the scene you model is more urban, use buildings to disguise the gap. Building flats (one-sided buildings that are three-dimensional on the facade side) installed directly against the backdrop work really well. These buildings can have loading docks and such, with rail spurs serving the industries. Using flats is a great way to get more business for the railroad without modeling the whole buildings.

Combine these building flats

with commercially available backdrops of cities or urban scenes to further enhance the illusion. When you use these city backdrops, sometimes it is best just to use the portions that work well for your railroad. Cut out the buildings you need and overlap them, if it works. By cutting them out, you keep the sky color of your own backdrop, and you don't have to deal with any seams.

I have used color pencils and cardstock to draw the buildings that were necessary for a certain scene. Buy some decent colored

pencils, ones that will be rich in color and opaque, at an art supply store. Sketch the building on paper at about the size you need. Test-fit this mockup in place on the layout to see if it fits. Once you have determined the size, draw the building on a piece of cardstock using a straightedge and sharp colored pencils. You can use ink too, but it doesn't work well over the colored pencils. You can draw the building at the workbench, which is a lot easier than trying to draw it on the backdrop of the layout. When you're

The finished model fits nicely into the corner off the balloon loop. The viewer can hardly see that half of the building doesn't exist.

finished, cut out the building and install it directly onto the backdrop. You can use glue or even tape for easy removal in the future. This way to build flats works especially well if you are trying to replicate a certain building that is in the prototype scene.

Three-dimensional buildings

A building doesn't have to be two-dimensional to hide the seam between the scenery and backdrop. A three-dimensional model can easily be flush with the backdrop to hide the edge. I have even custom-built a building that was not parallel to the backdrop.

A feed mill was located on the balloon loop at Durango, Colorado, on the Denver and Rio Grande Western narrow gauge. In our model of Durango, this mill was perfect as an industry that could be served by the railroad. There wasn't much room in this area because of its close proximity to the backdrop. And because of the curved nature of the balloon loop, an industry flat against the backdrop would not work too well, either.

I decided to try building a portion of a building on an angle against the backdrop, with the back half missing. The completed building fit perfectly in the corner of the layout, and I built a short spur off the loop. The only part of the model that reveals that it is missing the back half is a slightly strange angle to the upper roof line. But overall, the building works well to hide the seam between the scenery and the backdrop. I have built a few other buildings that do the same thing, and I never miss the part that isn't there.

Using scenery in the transition

Sometimes the best way to hide the seam is to use more scenery. You can use lots of trees, of course. But you can even use rockwork and other scenery materials. Thin slices of insulation foam, carved to resemble rocks and glued directly to the backdrop, work really well. Plaster castings work too, but often they are not flat enough or too brittle.

A group of buildings and trees can draw the eye away from the backdrop enough to disguise the gap. Just make sure the scenery is built up all the way to the

Left: A model of a feed mill at Durango on the HOn3 of Herb and Mike Danneman Right: Modeling the back half of this feed mill was not necessary, since it butts against the backdrop

Top left: Two SP SD45s exit a tunnel in this N scale scene. The backdrop is only an inch or so from the train. A thin piece of insulation foam carved into rock shapes and glued to the backdrop forms the rocky outcrop above the UP boxcar.

Top right: Sometimes just a large group of structures and trees is a great way to hide the seam between the scenery and the backdrop.

Above right: Two Milwaukee, Racine & Troy SD40-2s roll through the open farm vistas of the Midwest. Here, scenery was built right up to the backdrop, and distant, golden fields were painted on the backdrop. A smattering of simple building forms to simulate clusters of farm buildings finished the scene. No attempt was made to blend the end of the scenery into the backdrop, since the scenery represents rolling hills with a view into a valley.

backdrop, and complete the rest of the scenery details. As long as the colors of the scenery are close in tone to those on the backdrop, the structures and other details will hide the joint.

Sometimes, just the rolling scenery butted flush against the backdrop with more scenery painted on the backdrop is enough to provide the illusion of space. As long as the background scenery is lighter and bluer to resemble something farther away, the illusion will work. Try using any method available, depending on the type of scenery near the backdrop.

Helpful Hint #2   Take a scene like this one on the Santa Fe main line in the desert at Fenner, California. How would you hide a seam between the scenery and backdrop on a model of this? See old Route 66 cruising along the main right behind the train? Butt the highway right up to the backdrop. Everything from the highway forward is three-dimensional. Everything past the highway is painted on the backdrop. The straight-as-an-arrow Route 66 makes a perfect and simple place to put the transition. And don't forget to get that old brush out to stipple all those desert plants onto the backdrop.

After all the work you have done on the scenery and back-drop, you might think the layout is about finished. But what is so much fun about model railroading is that the layout is never truly finished. There are always more trees to add, or structures to build. And scenic detailing can be endless. Try adding more figures, animals, and vehicles to your layout. They are as much a part of scenery as anything. Adding some mini-scenes to your layout can also add just the right amount of scenic detail to make the layout come alive.

Right: Look at the detail of this street scene by Bill and Wayne Reid! It shows a local Pennsylvania freight backing down Railroad Avenue in Shippensburg, Pennsylvania, to make a pickup at Cumberland Valley Bakery. The signs, people, vehicles, sidewalks, and street-running all combine to give this scene a wealth of detail. And all of this is in N scale!

Below right: An eastbound BN freight east of Bison, Montana, heads through a nice scene of mountains, evergreens, autumn color, and a field of grass. The simple addition of a pair of horses makes this scene complete.

Wayne Reid

Top: Vehicles should be weathered to various degrees, just like the rolling stock. Look at that beat-up and rusty Chevy next to the station. And don't forget to weather some of the figures' clothing to give them that dirty "I've been workin' on the railroad" look.

Above: Three mountain climbers are scaling some cliffs in this scene. Not all figures have to be working on or near the railroad. Isolate some into their own little mini-scenes.

Left: Two Western Maryland freights meet in Shippensburg, Pennsylvania, on the Reid brothers' N scale layout. Details like the retaining walls and the chain-link fence around Franklin County Power and Light bring the scene to life.

Above: Various degrees of weathering and scenery on and around the track can help define how well used it is. Many times our model track looks only like the top example. The track deserves some scenic detailing too.

Right: Sometimes real life can emulate models, as in this scene of Harpers Ferry, West Virginia. Tight and steeply graded streets, lots of vehicles, and beautiful old structures make this scene look almost model-like. And there is a train visible, an eastbound CSX freight.

Below right: Sometimes the mini-scene can be as simple as a small creek with a culvert or two under the main line, as in this prototype scene of a Wisconsin and Southern freight.